The Gospel of Judas

The Man, His History, His Story

Joseph B. Lumpkin

Joseph B. Lumpkin

Fifth Estate Publishers,

Post Office Box 116, Blountsville, AL 35031.

First Printing 2007

Printed on acid-free paper

Library of Congress Control No: 2007904842

ISBN 9781933580401

Cover design by An Quigley

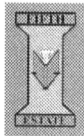

Fifth Estate

2007

Joseph B. Lumpkin

The Question of Judas

No discovery since the Dead Sea Scrolls has rocked the Christian world like that of the newly translated "Gospel of Judas." The story presented in the short but powerful text reveals a plan in which heavenly ends justified monstrous means. Betrayal became collaboration and murder resembled suicide as Jesus and Judas began a macabre dance into eternity.

Orthodox Christianity has its doctrine, its canon, and its political story, but these are quite different from those exposed in the Gospel of Judas.

As the orthodox political viewpoint would have it, Jesus' demise was sought by the Roman authorities as he gained a following and was declared "King" by the Jewish populace. The Jewish religious leaders were also planning his death, believing that Jesus was attempting to reform Judaism, and wrest their control over the people.

The Gospel of Judas calls into question this accepted view of the political intrigue leading up to Jesus' betrayal and death.

Spokesman for the Maecenas Foundation, one of the companies in Basel, Switzerland working on the Judas project, Director Mario Jean Roberty, reports:

"We have just received the results of carbon dating: the text is older than we thought and dates back to a period between the beginning of the third and fourth centuries. We do not want to reveal the exceptional side of what we have, except that the Judas Iscariot text called into question some of the political principles of Christian doctrine."

Imagine Judas, the man all of Christendom has hated for two thousand years, now portrayed as the chosen one, the martyr, the scapegoat, and the man instructed and appointed by Jesus himself to orchestrate and carry out the greatest treachery of all time. But treachery ordered by the one betrayed is not treachery at all, but a loyal and devoted follower carrying out the wishes of his master.

What was Judas' reward for betraying Jesus? According to the Gospel of Judas it was special recognition by God and the blessing of Jesus, the savior of mankind. Strangely, there is evidence in our own Bible to substantiate this claim. Judas may have been promised a position of authority along with the other apostles.

The Gospel of Judas turns us on our heads and forces upon the reader a new and uncomfortable view. Did Judas have special knowledge and instruction from Jesus?

Are we to thank him for the death of Jesus? Is lethal treachery appointed by the victim suicide or murder? Is this murderous quisling really a saint?

Who is this man, Judas? What do we know about him? Where did he come from? What did he want? What did he do?

These are just a few of the questions left to reverberate in the mind of the reader.

Theories of Judas abound. He is presented as greedy and selfish as well as sanctified spirit. Some say he was possessed, some say he was a saint, and some believe him to be Satan himself.

Was Judas the impetus of death, burial, and resurrection for Jesus, and thus the daemon who saved us? Will Judas be the Antichrist we will meet in the end of days or will he be ruling and judging the tribes of Israel?

Every story has two sides. Let us examine both sides, beginning with The Gospel of Judas, its history, its theology, and its text.

Understanding the Intent

The Gospel of Judas can be understood on a deeper level if its background is explored first.

One may ask the proper questions regarding the text of "who, what, when, where, and why." The question of "who" wrote the Gospel of Judas we might never know. What the author was trying to say will be explored in depth. Science can and has narrowed down the "when" and "where."

Why mankind writes is axiomatic. We write to document, explain, express, or convince. In the end, those are the reasons. Time will tell if the author of Judas has succeeded.

In a time when Gnosticism was struggling for influence in Christendom, the Gospel of Judas was written to challenge the beliefs of the newly emerging church orthodoxy, to explain Gnostic theology, and to propagate the sect. To better understand the gospel, it must be read with these goals in mind.

For centuries the definition of Gnosticism has in itself been a point of confusion and contention within the religious community. This is due in part to the ever-broadening application of the term and the fact that various sects of Gnosticism existed as the theology evolved and began to merge into what became mainstream Christianity.

Even though Gnosticism continued to evolve, it is the theology in place at the time that the Gospel of Judas was written that should be considered and understood before attempting to render or read a translation. To do otherwise would make the translation cloudy and obtuse.

It becomes the duty of both translator and reader to understand the ideas being espoused and the terms conveying those ideas. A grasp of theology, cosmology, and relevant terms is necessary for a clear transmission of the meaning within the text in question.

With this in mind, we will briefly examine Gnostic theology, cosmology, and history. We will focus primarily on Gnostic sects existing in the first through fourth centuries A.D. since it is believed most Gnostic Gospels were written during that time. It was also during that time that reactions within the emerging Christian orthodoxy began to intensify and the Gospel of Judas was written.

The downfall of many books written on the topic of religion is the attempt to somehow remove history and people from the equation. History shapes religion because it shapes the perception and direction of religious leaders.

Religion also develops and evolves in an attempt to make sense of the universe as it is seen and understood at the time. Thus, to truly grasp a religious concept it is important to know the history, people, and cosmology of the time. These areas are not separate but are continually interacting.

What is the Gospel of Judas?

What is the Gospel of Judas and why does it differ so greatly from the gospel stories of the Bible?

The Gospel of Judas is considered a Gnostic text. The Gnostics were a sect of Christianity and like any sect or religion, they were fighting to expand and continue under the persecution of the newly emerging orthodoxy of the day.

The Gospel of Judas may have been written to help bolster and continue Gnosticism. This may explain its radical departure from the traditional Gospel story, as well as the reason for its creation.

Indeed, one way of looking at any religious book, canon or not, is as an attempt to explain one's beliefs, to persuade others toward those beliefs, and to interpret history and known storylines in the light of one's own theology and cosmology. This is done not only to add weight to one's own belief system but also simply because man sees events as having relevance to what he or she holds as truth.

As previously stated, the Gospel of Judas is, above all things, a Gnostic gospel since it revolves around a special knowledge or Gnosis given to Judas by Jesus. This knowledge represented that which Gnostics held as the universal truth. But what is Gnosticism?

11

The roots of the Gnosticism may pre-date Christianity. Similarities exist between Gnosticism and the wisdom and mystery cults found in Egypt and Greece. Gnosticism contains the basic terms and motifs of Plato's cosmology as well as the mystical qualities of Pythagorean cosmology and Buddhism. All of this was mixed with the Christianity of the second and third centuries to form the Gnosticism that is offered in the Gospel of Judas.

Plato was steeped in Greek mythology, and the Gnostic creation myth has elements owing to this. Both cosmology and mysticism within Gnosticism present an interpretation of Christ's existence and teachings, thus, Gnostics are considered to be a Christian sect.

Gnostic followers are urged to look within themselves for the truth and the Christ spirit hidden, asleep in their souls. The battle cry can be summed up in the words of the Gnostic Gospel of Thomas, verse 3:

Jesus said: If those who lead you say to you: Look, the Kingdom is in the sky, then the birds of the sky would enter before you. If they say to you: It is in the sea, then the fish of the sea would enter ahead of you. But the Kingdom of God exists within you and it exists outside of you. Those who come to know (recognize) themselves will find it, and when you come to know yourselves you will become known and you will realize that you are the children of the Living Father. Yet if you do not come to know yourselves then you will dwell in poverty and it will be you who are that poverty.

Paganism was a religious, traditional society in the Mediterranean leading up to the time of the Gnostics. Centuries after the conversion of Constantine, mystery cults worshipping various Egyptian and Greco-Roman gods continued. These cults taught that through their secret knowledge worshippers could control or escape the mortal realm. The Gnostic doctrine of inner knowledge and freedom may have part of its roots here. The concept of duality and inner guidance taught in Buddhism added to and enforced Gnostic beliefs, as we will see later.

The belief systems of Plato, Buddha, and paganism melded together, spread, and found a suitable home in the mystical side of the Christian faith as it sought to adapt and adopt certain Judeo-Christian beliefs and symbols.

Like modern Christianity, Gnosticism had various points of view that could be likened to Christian denominations of today. Complex and elaborate creation myths took root in Gnosticism, being derived from those of Plato. Later, the theology evolved and Gnosticism began to shed some of its more unorthodox myths, leaving the central theme of inner knowledge or "gnosis" as the path to enlightenment and salvation. In Gnosticism it is knowledge that saves one from hell fire. This knowledge and its place in man's salvation was their message to propagate. Exactly what the knowledge was and how is was expressed seemed to vary between Gnostic sects.

The existence of various sects of Gnosticism, differing creation stories, along with the lack of historical documentation, has left scholars in a quandary about exactly what Gnostics believed.

Although it appears that there were several sects of Gnosticism, we will attempt to discuss the more universal Gnostic beliefs along with the highlights of the major sects.

Gnostic cosmology, (which is the theory of how the universe is created, constructed, and sustained), is complex and very different from orthodox Christianity cosmology. In many ways Gnosticism may appear to be polytheistic or even pantheistic.

To understand some of the basic beliefs of Gnosticism, let us start with the common ground shared between Gnosticism and modern Christianity. Both believe the world is imperfect, corrupt, and brutal. The blame for this, according to mainstream Christianity, is placed squarely on the shoulders of man himself. With the fall of man (Adam), the world was forever changed to the undesirable and harmful place in which we live today. However, Gnostics reject this view as an incorrect interpretation of the creation myth.

According to Gnostics, the blame is not in us, but in our creator. The creator of this world was himself somewhat less than perfect and in fact, deeply flawed and cruel, making mankind the children of a lesser God. It is in the book, *The Apocryphon of John* that the Gnostic view of creation is presented to us in great detail.

Gnosticism also teaches that in the beginning a Supreme Being called The Father, The Divine All, The Origin, The Supreme God, or The Fullness, emanated the element of existence, both visible and invisible. His intent was not to create but, just as light emanates from a flame, so did creation shine forth from God. This manifested the primal element needed for creation. This was the creation of Barbelo, who is the Thought of God.

The Father's thought performed a deed and she was created from it. It is she who had appeared before him in the shining of his light. This is the first power which was before all of them and which was created from his mind. She is the Thought of the All and her light shines like his light. It is the perfect power which is the visage of the invisible. She is the pure, undefiled Spirit who is perfect. She is the first power, the glory of Barbelo, the perfect glory of the kingdom (kingdoms), the glory revealed. She glorified the pure, undefiled Spirit and it was she who praised him, because thanks to him she had come forth.

     The Apocryphon of John

It could be said that Barbelo was the creative emanation and, like the Divine All, is both male and female. It was the "agreement" of Barbelo and the Divine All, representing the union of male and female, that created the Christ Spirit and all the Aeons. In some renderings the word "Aeon" is used to designate an ethereal realm or kingdom. In other versions "Aeon" indicates the ruler of the realm. The Aeons of this world are merely reflections of the Aeons of the eternal realm. The reflection is always inferior to real. This idea is of Aeons above and below, the real and reflected, the superior and inferior is brought up in the Gospel of Judas. Barbelo is mentioned by name in Judas. Another of these rulers was called Sophia or Wisdom. Her fall began a chain of events that led to the introduction of evil into the universe.

Seeing the Divine flame of God, Sophia sought to know its origin. She sought to know the very nature of God. Sophia's passion ended in tragedy when she managed to capture a divine and creative spark, which she attempted to duplicate with her own creative force, without the union of a male counterpart. It was this act that produced the Archons, beings born outside the higher divine realm. In the development of the myth, explanations seem to point to the fact that Sophia carried the divine essence of creation from God within her but chose to attempt creation by using her own powers. It is unclear if this was in an attempt to understand the Supreme God and his power, or an impetuous act that caused evil to enter the cosmos in the form of her creations.

The realm containing the Fullness of the Godhead and Sophia is called the pleroma or Realm of Fullness. This is the Gnostic heaven. The lesser Gods created in Sophia's failed attempt were cast outside the pleroma and away from the presence of God. In essence, she threw away and discarded her flawed creations.

"She cast it away from her, outside the place where no one of the immortals might see it, for she had created it in ignorance. And she surrounded it with a glowing cloud, and she put a throne in the middle of the cloud so that no one could see it except the Holy Spirit who is called the mother of all that has life. And she called his name Yaldaboth."

Apocryphon of John

The beings Sophia created were imperfect and oblivious to the Supreme God. Her creations contained deities even less perfect than herself. They were called the Powers, the Rulers, or the Archons. Their leader was called the Demiurge, but his name was Yaldaboth, also spelled "Yaldabaoth." It was the flawed, imperfect, spiritually blind Demiurge, (Yaldaboth), who became the creator of the material world and all things in it. Gnostics considered Yaldaboth to be the same as Jehovah (Yahweh), who is the Jewish creator God. These beings, the Demiurge and the Archons, would later equate to Satan and his demons, or Jehovah and his angels, depending on which Gnostic sect is telling the story. Both are equally evil.

In one Gnostic creation story, the Archons created Adam but could not bring him to life. In other stories Adam was formed as a type of worm, unable to attain personhood.

Thus, man began as an incomplete creation of a flawed, spiritually blind, and malevolent god. In this myth, the Archons were afraid that Adam might be more powerful than the Archons themselves. When they saw Adam was incapable of attaining the human state, their fears were put to rest, thus, they called that day the "Day of Rest."

Sophia saw Adam's horrid state and had compassion, because she knew she was the origin of the Archons and their evil. Sophia descended to help bring Adam out of his hopeless condition. It is this story that set the stage for the emergence of the sacred feminine force in Gnosticism that is not seen in orthodox Christianity. Sophia brought within herself the light and power of the Supreme God. Metaphorically, within the spiritual womb of Sophia was carried the life force of the Supreme God for Adam's salvation.

In the Gnostic text, *The Apocryphon of John*, Sophia is quoted:

"I entered into the midst of the cage which is the prison of the body. And I spoke saying: 'He who hears, let him awake from his deep sleep.' Then Adam wept and shed tears. After he wiped away his bitter tears he

asked: 'Who calls my name, and from where has this hope arose in me even while I am in the chains of this prison?' And I (Sophia) answered: 'I am the one who carries the pure light; I am the thought of the undefiled spirit. Arise, remember, and follow your origin, which is I, and beware of the deep sleep.'"

Sophia would later equate to the Holy Spirit as it awakened the comatose soul.

As the myth evolved, Sophia, after animating Adam, became Eve in order to assist Adam in finding the truth. She offered it to him in the form of the fruit of the tree of knowledge. To Gnostics, this was an act of deliverance.

Other stories have Sophia becoming the serpent in order to offer Adam a way to attain the truth. In either case, the apple represented the hard sought truth, which was the knowledge of good and evil, and through that knowledge Adam could become a god. Later, the serpent would become a feminine symbol of wisdom, probably owing to the connection with Sophia. Eve, being Sophia in disguise, would become the mother and sacred feminine of us all. As Gnostic theology began to coalesce, Sophia would come to be considered a force or conduit of the Holy Spirit, in part due to the fact that the Holy Spirit was also considered a feminine and creative force from the Supreme God. The Gospel of Philip echoes this theology in verse six as follows:

> *In the days when we were Hebrews we were made orphans, having only our Mother. Yet when we believed in the Messiah (and became the ones of Christ), the Mother and Father both came to us.*
> *Gospel of Philip*

As the emerging orthodox church became more and more oppressive to women, later even labeling them "occasions of sin," the Gnostics countered by raising women to equal status with men, saying Sophia was, in a sense, the handmaiden or wife of the Supreme God, making the soul of Adam her spiritual offspring. But, the placement and purpose of Sophia, Barbelo, Yaldaboth, and other deities vary somewhat from one type of Gnosticism to another.

In several Gnostic cosmologies the "living" world is under the control of entities called Aeons, of which Sophia is head. This means the Aeons influence or control the soul, life force, intelligence, thought, and mind. Control of the mechanical or inorganic world is given to the

21

Archons. They rule the physical aspects of systems, regulation, limits, and order in the world. Both the ineptitude and cruelty of the Archons are reflected in the chaos and pain of the material realm.

The lesser God that created the world, Yaldaboth began his existence in a state that was both detached and remote from the Supreme God in aspects both spiritual and physical. Since Sophia had misused her creative force, which passed from the Supreme God (some say, through Barbelo) to her, Sophia's creation, the Demiurge, or Yaldaboth, contained only part of the original creative spark of the Supreme Being. He was created with an imperfect nature caused by his distance in lineage and in spirit from the Divine All or Supreme God. It is because of his imperfections and limited abilities the lesser God is also called the "Half-Maker."

The Creator God, the Demiurge, and his helpers, the Archons took the stuff of existence produced by the Supreme God and fashioned it into this material world.

Since the Demiurge (Yaldaboth) had no memory of how he came to be alive, he did not realize he was not the true creator. The Demiurge believed he somehow came to create the material world by himself. The Supreme God allowed the Demiurge and Archons to remain deceived.

The Creator God (the Demiurge) intended the material world to be perfect and eternal, but he did not have it in himself to accomplish the feat. What comes forth from a being cannot be greater than the highest part of him, can it? The world was created flawed and transitory and we are part of it. Can we escape? The Demiurge was imperfect and evil. So was the world he created. If it was the Demiurge who created man and man is called upon to escape the Demiurge and find union with the Supreme God, is this not demanding that man becomes greater than his creator? Spiritually this seems impossible, but as many children become greater than their parents, man is expected to become greater than his maker, the Demiurge. This starts with the one fact that the Demiurge denies the existence and supremacy of the Supreme God, but through gnosis man rises above this blindness.

Man was created with a dual nature as the product of the material world of the Demiurge with his imperfect essence, combined with the spark of God that emanated from the Supreme God through Sophia. A version of the creation story has Sophia instructing the Demiurge to breathe into Adam that spiritual power he had taken from Sophia during his creation. It was the spiritual power from Sophia that brought life to Adam.

It is this divine spark in man that calls to its source, the Supreme God, and which causes a "divine discontent," that nagging feeling that keeps us questioning if this is all there is. This spark and the feeling it gives us keeps us searching for the truth.

The Creator God sought to keep man ignorant of his defective state by keeping him enslaved to the material world. By doing so, he continued to receive man's worship and servitude. He did not wish man to recognize or gain knowledge of the true Supreme God. Since he did not know or acknowledge the Supreme God, he views any attempt to worship anything else as spiritual treason.

The opposition of forces set forth in the spiritual battle over the continued enslavement of man and man's spiritual freedom set up the duality of good and evil in Gnostic theology. There was a glaring difference between the orthodox Christian viewpoint and the Gnostic viewpoint. According to Gnostics, the creator of the material world was an evil entity and the Supreme God, who was his source, was the good entity. Christians quote John 1:1 "In the beginning was the Word, and the Word was with God, and the Word was God."

According to Gnostics, only through the realization of man's true state or through death can he escape captivity in the material realm. This means the idea of salvation does not deal with original sin or blood payment. Instead, it focuses on the idea of awakening to the fullness of the truth.

According to Gnostic theology, neither Jesus nor his death can save anyone, but the truth that he came to proclaim can allow a person to save his or her own soul. It is the truth, or realization of the lie of the material world and its God, that sets one on a course of freedom. It cannot be overstated that in the eyes of many Gnostics, the death of Jesus was part of a plan implemented to show men in metaphorical terms the lack of worth and permanence of the physical world as opposed to the spiritual. The physical death of Jesus could not save us in the way orthodox Christianity came to understand it. His death was not a sacrifice to pay for our sins, but instead it was more of a lesson by example of the fight and plight of the temporal world which was at war with the eternal world.

To escape the earthly prison and find one's way back to the pleroma (heaven) and the Supreme God, is the soteriology (salvation doctrine) and eschatology (judgment, reward, and doctrine of heaven) of Gnosticism.

The idea that personal revelation leads to salvation may be what caused the mainline Christian church to declare Gnosticism a heresy. The church could better tolerate alternative theological views if the views did not undermine the authority of the church and its ability to control the people. Gnostic theology placed salvation in the hands of the individual through personal revelations and knowledge, excluding the need for the orthodox church and its clergy to grant salvation or absolution. This fact, along with the divergent interpretation of the creation story, which placed the creator God, Yaldaboth or Jehovah, as the enemy of mankind, was too much for the church to tolerate. Reaction was harsh. Gnosticism was declared to be a dangerous heresy.

Gnosticism may be considered polytheistic because it espoused many "levels" of Gods, beginning with an ultimate, unknowable, Supreme God and descending as he created Sophia, and Sophia created the Demiurge (Creator God); each becoming more inferior and limited.

There is a hint of pantheism in Gnostic theology due to the fact that creation occurs because of a deterioration of the Godhead and the dispersion of the creative essence, which eventually devolves into the creation of man.

In the end, there occurs a universal reconciliation as being after being realizes the existence of the Supreme God and renounces the material world and its inferior creator.

Combined with its Christian influences, the cosmology of the Gnostics may have borrowed from the Greek philosopher, Plato, as well as from Pythagoras and even Buddhism. There are disturbing parallels between the creation myth set forth by Plato and some of those recorded in Gnostic writings.

Pythagoras was born on the island of Samos between 580 and 570 B.C. His father is thought to have been a gem-engraver, and it is likely that the son would have been trained in that same craft.

Some scholars report that he was the first man to call himself and philosopher, or "lover of wisdom." Indeed, many of the accomplishments of such great men as Plato, Aristotle, and even Copernicus were based on the work of Pythagoras.

Pythagoras believed in Orphism, which is a theology that taught the soul and body are united but unequal. The soul is divine, immortal, and eternal. Its original state was one of freedom, before being imprisoned in a body. The body holds it imprisoned but death frees the soul, although only for a while. The soul is destined to be imprisoned again and again as the cycle of birth and death revolves until the end of time.

The soul journeys through its existence alternating

from freedom to capture through reincarnations, as it learns lessons through many bodies of men and animals. The earliest Greek we can connect to Orphism is the sixth century thinker, Pherecydes. Pythagoras was his pupil and the individual most responsible for spreading Orphism throughout Greece.

Pythagoras further developed his beliefs while visiting Egypt, Greece, and Tyre in Lebanon. During his visit to Tyre he was initiated for the first time into the 'Ancient Mysteries' of the Phoenicians and studied for about 3 years in the temples of Tyre, Sidon, and Byblos.

It was after years of study that Pythagoras founded the famous Pythagorean School of philosophy, mathematics, and natural sciences. There he taught a simple lifestyle was best. Modesty, austerity, patience, and self-control were stressed. They consumed vegetarian, dried and condensed food, and unleavened bread. They did not cut their hair, beard, and nails.

The Pythagoreans believed that the universe could be understood in terms of whole numbers. This belief stemmed from observations in music, mathematics, and astronomy. He once commented, "Number is the ruler of form and the ideas and cause of gods and demons." We will see that symbolism of number plays a large part in The

Gospel of Judas.

The Pythagoreans taught the doctrine of transmigration of souls, which states that after death, a man's soul enters the body of a newborn infant or animal and so lives another life. The soul wanders from the home of the blessed, being born into all kinds of corporeal forms as it travels from one path of life to another.

One of his students wrote, "I am also one of these, an exile and a wanderer from the Gods. Ere now, I too have been a boy, a girl, a bush, a bird, and a scaly fish in the sea."
- Empedocles

Their cosmology conceived of a universe made of numbers. There were four major numbers and meanings making up all we see: one for a point, two for a line, three for a surface, and four for a solid. One was the basis, and generated the series of even and odd numbers, and with them the whole universe. Moral qualities were numbers: 4 (2x2 and 2+2) was justice, equal shares all round. A special number was 10, built up of 1+2+3+4, and containing the point, line, plane, and solid. This sequence was known as the *tetractys*. *Followers swore* an oath not to reveal the mysteries of the society 'by Him who reveals Himself to our minds in the Tetractys, which contains the source and roots of everlasting nature'.

Pythagoras had also discovered the mathematical basis of music, and the fact that the relation halves can express an octave. A string stopped at half its length will vibrate to give the sound of the octave above the full length. So music was involved in all life; and even the planets circling in their courses sounded the music of the spheres.

Plato lived from 427 to 347 B.C. He was the son of wealthy Athenians and a student of the philosopher, Socrates, and the mathematician, Pythagoras. Plato himself was the teacher of Aristotle.

In Plato's cosmology, the Demiurge was an artist who imposed form on materials that already existed. The raw materials were in a chaotic and random state. The physical world must have had visible form which was put together in a fashion much like a puzzle is constructed. This later gave way to a philosophy which stated that all things in existence could be broken down into a small subset of geometric shapes.

In the tradition of Greek mythology, Plato's cosmology began with a creation story. The story was narrated by the philosopher Timaeus of Locris, a fictional character of Plato's making. In his account, nature is initiated by a creator deity, called the "Demiurge," a name which may be the Geek word for "craftsman" or "artisan" or, according to how one divides the word, it could also be translated as "half-maker."

The Demiurge sought to create the cosmos modeled on his understanding of the supreme and original truth. In this way he created the visible universe based on invisible truths. He set in place rules of process such as birth, growth, change, death, and dissolution. This was Plato's "Realm of Becoming." It was his Genesis. Plato stated that the internal structure of the cosmos had innate intelligence and was therefore called the World Soul. The cosmic super-structure of the Demiurge was used as the framework on which to hang or fill in the details and parts of the universe. The Demiurge then appointed his underlings to fill in the details, which allowed the universe to remain in a working and balanced state. All phenomena of nature resulted from an interaction and interplay of the two forces of reason and necessity.

Plato represented reason as constituting the World Soul. The material world was a necessity in which reason acted out its will in the physical realm. The duality between the will, mind, or reason of the World Soul and the material universe and its inherent flaws set in play the duality of Plato's world and is seen reflected in the beliefs of the Gnostics.

31

In Plato's world, the human soul was immortal, each soul was assigned to a star. Souls that were just or good were permitted to return to their stars upon their death to rest and dwell there in peace. Unjust souls were reincarnated to try again. Escape of the soul to the freedom of the stars and out of the cycle of reincarnation was best accomplished by following the reason and goodness of the World Soul and not the physical world, which was set in place only as a necessity to manifest the patterns of the World Soul.

Although in Plato's cosmology the Demiurge was not seen as evil, in Gnostic cosmology he was considered not only to be flawed and evil, but he was also the beginning of all evil in the material universe, having created it to reflect his own malice.

Following the path of Pythagoras and Plato's cosmology, some Gnostics left open the possibility of reincarnation if the person had not reached the truth before his death. This idea of the transmigration of the soul may have been linked to influences from the East.

In the year 13 A.D. Roman annals record the visit of an Indian king named Pandya or Porus. He came to see Caesar Augustus carrying a letter of introduction in Greek. He was accompanied by a monk who burned himself alive in the city of Athens to prove his faith in Buddhism. The event was described by Nicolaus of Damascus as, not surprisingly, causing a great stir among the people. It is thought that this was the first transmission of Buddhist teaching to the masses.

In the second century A.D., Clement of Alexandria wrote about Buddha: "Among the Indians are those philosophers also who follow the precepts of Boutta (Buddha), whom they honour as a god on account of his extraordinary sanctity." (Clement of Alexandria, "The Stromata, or Miscellanies" Book I, Chapter XV).

"Thus philosophy, a thing of the highest utility, flourished in antiquity among the barbarians, shedding its light over the nations. And afterwards it came to Greece." Clement of Alexandria, "The Stromata, or Miscellanies".

To clarify what "philosophy" was transmitted from India to Greece, we turn to the historians Hippolytus and Epiphanius who wrote of Scythianus, a man who had visited India around 50 A.D. They report; "He brought 'the doctrine of the Two Principles.'" According to these writers, Scythianus' pupil Terebinthus called himself a Buddha. Some scholars suggest it was he that traveled to the area of Babylon and transmitted his knowledge to Mani, who later founded Manichaeism.

Adding to the possibility of Eastern influence, we have accounts of the Apostle Thomas' attempt to convert the people of Asia-Minor. If the Gnostic gospel bearing his name was truly written by Thomas, it was penned after his return from India, where he also encountered the Buddhist influences.

Following the transmission of the philosophy of "Two Principals," both Manichaeism and Gnosticism retained a dualistic viewpoint. The black-versus-white dualism of Gnosticism came to rest in the evil of the material world and its maker, versus the goodness of the freed soul and the Supreme God with whom it seeks union.

Oddly, the disdain for the material world and its Creator God drove Gnostic theology to far-flung extremes in attitude, beliefs, and actions. Gnostics idolized the serpent in the "Garden of Eden" story. After all, if your salvation hinges on secret knowledge, the offer of becoming gods through the knowledge of good and evil sounds wonderful. So powerful was the draw of this "knowledge myth" to the Gnostics that the serpent became linked to Sophia by some sects. This can still be seen today in our medical and veterinarian symbols of serpents on poles, conveying the ancient meanings of knowledge and wisdom.

Genesis 3 (King James Version)

1 Now the serpent was more subtil than any beast of the field which the LORD God had made. And he said unto the woman, Yea, hath God said, Ye shall not eat of every tree of the garden?

2 And the woman said unto the serpent, We may eat of the fruit of the trees of the garden:

3 But of the fruit of the tree which is in the midst of the garden, God hath said, Ye shall not eat of it, neither shall ye touch it, lest ye die.

4 And the serpent said unto the woman, Ye shall not surely die:

5 For God doth know that in the day ye eat thereof, then your eyes shall be opened, and ye shall be as Gods, knowing good and evil.

It is because of their vehement struggle against the Creator God and the search for some transcendent truth, that Gnostics held the people of Sodom in high regard. The people of Sodom sought to "corrupt" the messengers sent by their enemy, the Creator God. Anything done to thwart the Demiurge and his minions was considered valiant.

Genesis 19 (King James Version)

1 And there came two angels to Sodom at even; and Lot sat in the gate of Sodom: and Lot seeing them rose up to meet them; and he bowed himself with his face toward the ground;

2 And he said, Behold now, my lords, turn in, I pray you, into your servant's house, and tarry all night, and wash your feet, and ye shall rise up early, and go on your ways. And they said, Nay; but we will abide in the street all night.

3 And he pressed upon them greatly; and they turned in unto him, and entered into his house; and he made them a feast, and did bake unleavened bread, and they did eat.

4 But before they lay down, the men of the city, even the men of Sodom, compassed the house round, both old and young, all the people from every quarter:

5 And they called unto Lot, and said unto him, Where are the men which came in to thee this night? bring them out unto us, that we may know them.

6 And Lot went out at the door unto them, and shut the door after him,

7 And said, I pray you, brethren, do not so wickedly.

8 Behold now, I have two daughters which have not known man; let me, I pray you, bring them out unto you, and do ye to them as is good in your eyes: only unto these men do nothing; for therefore came they under the shadow of my roof.

9 And they said, Stand back. And they said again, This one fellow came in to sojourn, and he will needs be a judge: now will we deal worse with thee, than with them. And they pressed sore upon the man, even Lot, and came near to break the door.

10 But the men put forth their hand, and pulled Lot into the house to them, and shut to the door.

To modern Christians, the idea of admiring the serpent, which we believe was Satan, may seem unthinkable. Supporting the idea of attacking and molesting the angels sent to Sodom to warn of the coming destruction seems appalling; but to Gnostics the real evil was the malevolent entity, the Creator God of this world. To destroy his messengers, as was the case in Sodom, would impede his mission. To obtain knowledge of good and evil, as was offered by the serpent in the garden, would set the captives free.

The battle and highest call of Gnosticism was to awaken the inner knowledge of the true God. This is the God who is above and beyond that lower and evil god that created the material world. The material world was designed to prevent the awakening by entrapping, confusing, and distracting the spirit of man. The aim of Gnosticism was the spiritual awakening and freedom of man.

Gnostics, in the age of the early church, would preach to converts (novices) about this awakening, saying the novice must awaken the God within himself and see the trap that was the material world. Salvation came from the recognition or knowledge contained in this spiritual awakening. Moreover, it was the knowledge that the "illusion" of the material world existed and should be transcended that was the driving force and saving gnosis (knowledge) that Gnosticism was built upon.

Not all people were ready or willing to accept the Gnosis. Many were bound to the material world and satisfied to be only as and where they were. These have mistaken the Creator God for the Supreme God and do not know there is anything beyond the Creator God or the material existence. These people knew only the lower or earthly wisdom and not the higher wisdom above the Creator God. They were referred to as "dead."

Gnostic sects split primarily into two categories. Both branches held that those who were truly enlightened could no longer be influenced by the material world. Both divisions of Gnosticism believed that their spiritual journey could not be impeded by the material realm since the two were not only separate but in opposition. Such an attitude influenced some Gnostics toward Stoicism, choosing to abstain from the world, and others toward Epicureanism, choosing to indulge and satiate any and all appetites, since they believed the material world could not influence the spiritual world.

Major schools fell into two categories; those who rejected the material world of the Creator God, and those who rejected the laws of the Creator God. For those who rejected the world the Creator God had spawned, overcoming the material world was accomplished by partaking of as little of the world and its pleasures as possible. These followers lived very stark and ascetic lives, abstaining from meat, sex, marriage, and all things that would entice them to remain (or even wish to remain) in the material realm.

Other schools believed it was their duty to simply defy the Creator God and all laws that he had proclaimed. Since the Creator God had been identified as Jehovah, God of the Jews, these followers set about to break every law held dear by Christians and Jews.

As human nature is predisposed to do, many Gnostics took up the more wanton practices, believing that nothing done in their earthly bodies would affect their spiritual lives. Whether it was excesses in sex, alcohol, food, or any other assorted debaucheries, the Gnostics were safe within their faith, believing nothing spiritually bad could come of their earthly adventures.

Early Church leaders mention the actions of the Gnostics. One infamous Gnostic school is actually mentioned in the Bible, as we will read later.

The world was out of balance, inferior, and corrupt. The spirit was perfect and intact. It was up to the Gnostics to tell the story, explain the error, and awaken the world to the light of truth. The Supreme God had provided a vehicle to help in their effort. He had created a teacher of light and truth.

Since the time of Sophia's mistaken creation of the Archons, there was an imbalance in the cosmos. The Supreme God began to re-establish the balance by producing Christ to teach and save man. That left only Sophia, now in a fallen and bound state, along with the Demiurge, and the Archons to upset the cosmic equation. In this theology one might loosely equate the Supreme God to the New Testament Christian God, the Demiurge to Satan, the Archons to demons, the pleroma to heaven, and Sophia to the creative or regenerative force of the Holy Spirit.

This theory holds up well except for one huge problem. If the Jews believed that Jehovah created all things, and the Gnostic believed that the Demiurge created all things, then to the Gnostic mind, the Demiurge must be Old Testament god, Jehovah, and that made Jehovah their enemy. In this twist, the Old Testament God was the evil creator. The New Testament God was the true Supreme God, and Satan was a good and wise deity or savior, since he had offered a way of escape from the creator god when Satan offered the fruit of the tree of knowledge (or the Gnosis) to Eve.

For those who sought that which was beyond the material world and its flawed creator, the Supreme God sent Messengers of Light to awaken the divine spark of the Supreme God within us. This part of us will call to the True God as deep calls to deep. The greatest and most perfect

Messenger of Light was the Christ. He is also referred to as The Good, Christ, Messiah, and The Word. He came to reveal the Divine Light to mankind in the form of knowledge.

According to the Gnostics, Christ came to show us our own divine spark and to awaken us to the illusion of the material world and its flawed maker. He came to show us the way back to the divine Fullness (The Supreme God). The path to enlightenment was the knowledge sleeping within each of us. Christ came to show us the Christ spirit living in each of us. Individual ignorance or the refusal to awaken our internal divine spark was the only original sin. Christ was the only Word spoken by God that could awaken us. Christ was also the embodiment of the Word itself. He was part of the original transmission from the Supreme God that took form on the earth to awaken the soul of man so that man might search beyond the material world.

One Gnostic view of the Incarnation was "docetic," which is an early heretical position that Jesus was never actually present in the flesh, but only appeared to be human. He was a spiritual being and his human appearance was only an illusion. Of course, the title of "heretical" can only be decided by the controlling authority of the time. In this case it was the church that was about to emerge under the rule of the Emperor Constantine.

Most Gnostics held that the Christ spirit indwelt the earthly man, Jesus, at the time of his baptism by John, at which time Jesus received the name, and thus the power, of the Lord or Supreme God.

The Christ spirit departed from Jesus' body before his death. These two viewpoints remove the idea of God sacrificing himself as an atonement for the sins of man. The idea of atonement was not necessary in Gnostic theology since it was knowledge and not sacrifice that set one free.

Since there was a distinction in Gnosticism between the man Jesus and the Light of Christ that came to reside within him, it is not contrary to Gnostic beliefs that Mary Magdalene could have been the consort and wife of Jesus. Neither would it have been blasphemous for them to have had children.

Various sects of Gnosticism stressed certain elements of their basic theology. Each had its head teachers and its special flavor of beliefs. One of the oldest types was the Syrian Gnosticism. It existed around 120 A.D. In contrast to other sects, the Syrian lacked much of the embellished mythology of Aeons, Archons, and angels.

The fight between the Supreme God and the Creator God was not eternal, though there was strong opposition to Jehovah, the Creator God. He was considered to have been the last of the seven angels who created this world out of divine material which emanated from the Supreme God. The Demiurge attempted to create man, but only created a miserable worm which the Supreme God had to save by giving it the spark of divine life. Thus man was born.

According to this sect, Jehovah, the Creator God, must not be worshiped. The Supreme God calls man to his service and presence through Christ his Son. They pursued only the unknowable Supreme God and sought to obey the Supreme Deity by abstaining from eating meat and from marriage and sex, and by leading ascetic lives. The symbol of Christ was the serpent, who attempted to free Adam and Eve from their ignorance and entrapment to the Creator God.

Another Gnostic school was the Hellenistic or Alexandrian School. These systems absorbed the philosophy and concepts of the Greeks, and the Semitic nomenclature was replaced by Greek names. The cosmology and myth had grown out of proportion and appear to our eyes to be unwieldy. Yet, this school produced two great thinkers, Basilides and Valentinus. Though born at Antioch, in Syria, Basilides founded his school in Alexandria around the year A.D. 130, where it survived for several centuries.

Valentinus first taught at Alexandria and then in Rome. He established the largest Gnostic movement around A.D. 160. This movement was founded on an elaborate mythology and a system of sexual duality of male and female interplay, both in its deities and its savior.

Tertullian wrote that between 135 A.D. and 160 A.D. Valentinus, a prominent Gnostic, had great influence in the Christian church. Valentinus ascended in church hierarchy and became a candidate for the office of bishop of Rome, the office that quickly evolved into that of Pope. He lost the election by a narrow margin. Even though Valentinus was outspoken about his Gnostic slant on Christianity, he was a respected member of the Christian community until his death and was probably a practicing bishop in a church of lesser status than the one in Rome.

The main platform of Gnosticism was the ability to transcend the material world through the possession of privileged and directly imparted knowledge. Following this doctrine, Valentinus claimed to have been instructed by a direct disciple of one of Jesus' apostles, a man by the name of Theodas.

Joseph B. Lumpkin

Valentinus is considered by many to be the father of modern Gnosticism. His vision of the faith is summarized by G.R.S. Mead in the book "Fragments of a Faith Forgotten."

"The Gnosis in his hands is trying to embrace everything, even the most dogmatic formulation of the traditions of the Rabbi. The great popular movement and its incomprehensibilities were recognized by Valentinus as an integral part of the mighty outpouring; he laboured to weave all together, external and internal, into one piece, devoted his life to the task, and doubtless only at his death perceived that for that age he was attempting the impossible. None but the very few could ever appreciate the ideal of the man, much less understand it."

Fragments of a Faith Forgotten

The main stream of Gnosticism presented in the Gospel of Judas seems to be Sethian Gnosticism. Marvin Meyer, a respected scholar, describes Gospel of Judas as a Sethian Gnostic because it mentions the incorruptible generation of Seth and it shares common ideas with other

Sethian Gnostic writings found in the Nag Hammadi. The generation of Seth in Gnostic writings signified those born of the new generation of humanity after the tragic death of Abel and the banishment of Cain.

For Sethian Gnostics, Jesus was a teacher, "not a savior who dies for the sins of the world. For Gnostics, the fundamental problem in human life is not sin, but ignorance, and the best way to address this problem is not through faith, but through knowledge" (Meyer, Introduction to the Gospel of Judas [Washington, DC: National Geographic Society, 2006].

In the time period of the Gospel of Judas at about 180 A.D., Sethian Gnosticism had evolved by absorbing several basic doctrines: Hellenistic-Jewish mythology of Sophia, the divine wisdom; the midrashic interpretation of Genesis 1-6; a particular doctrine of baptism; the developing Christology of the early church; a religiously oriented view of Pythagorean metaphysics; and the teaching and philosophy of Plato including his theology and mythos regarding creation, Sophia, Barbelo, and the Creator God, Yalabaoth.

Sethian doctrines have baptism as a spiritualized ritual. In Sethian baptismal water was understood to be

47

"Living Water" identified with light or enlightenment and therefore salvation.

The history claimed by Sethian Gnosticism is derived from a peculiar exegesis of Genesis from a Jewish stand point. It should be stressed that the Sethian origins are not Christian but it absorbed Christian beliefs later. In their beginning they were looking for a messiah just as the Jews were, however, they believed he would be Seth. This is because they believed the imparted divine knowledge came down from God to Adam and was then transmitted to Seth.

Sethians adopted the rite of baptism often referred to as the Five-Seals. The ritual symbolized the removal of the person from the material world of the flesh and the ascension into the realm of light through the invocation of certain divine beings.

Sethianism began to change by its involvement in Christianity. This took place over time.

Sethianism was a non-Christian baptismal sect of the first centuries B.C.E. and C.E. which believed in enlightenment through knowledge by the divine wisdom which was that same wisdom that was revealed to Adam and Seth. It may be assumed that this was an incomplete passing of knowledge because the culmination was expected in a final visitation of Seth marked by his conferral of a saving baptism.

Baptism represented the descent of Seth as the living word or "Logos", which was bestowed through a holy baptism in the Living Water.

Barbelo, the Father-Mother god, who was a higher form of the Sophia figure, initiates those who were baptized in or by the Logos or Seth.

Barbelo communicated to those who love her by Voice or Word (Logos). This figure of Barbelo was the fountain or spring from which comes the Word like flowing water.

Protennoia is the Word or Logos, which was produced from Thought. The Word descends and enlightened her children.

The last of these entities was Eleleth who produces Sophia in the same way as fire produces light. The re-emission of this light through Sophia produced the demon Yaldaboth who stole the power of creation imparted to Sophia and produced the lower aeons and man.

The Archons thought that Protennoia (Logos) was "their Christ," while actually she is the "Father" of everyone. Protennoia identified herself as the beloved of the

Archons, and disguised herself as the child of the Great Creator.

Sethianism gradually Christianized in the latter first century as it began to identify Seth and Adam in terms of the pre-existent Christ.

This means that according to Sethian beliefs the true Son of Man is Adamas (Adam), the Son of the supreme deity who is the only human form in which the deity revealed himself. Seth, the son of Adam or Adamas, is the mediator between man and God's son, Adam. Seth was the Christ image or mediator.

Gnostic theology seemed to vacillate from polytheism to pantheism to dualism to monotheism, depending on the teacher and how he viewed and stressed certain areas of their creation myths.

Marcion, a Gnostic teacher, espoused differences between the God of the New Testament and the God of the Old Testament, claiming they were two separate entities. According to Marcion, the New Testament God was a good true God while the Old Testament God was an evil angel. Although this may be a heresy, it pulled his school back into monotheism. The church, however, disowned him.

Syneros and Prepon, disciples of Marcion, postulated three different entities, carrying their teachings from monotheism into polytheism in one stroke. In their system the opponent of the good God was not the God of the Jews, but Eternal Matter, which was the source of all evil. Matter, in this system became a principal creative force. Although it was created imperfect, it could also create, having the innate intelligence of the "world soul."

Of all the Gnostic schools or sects the most famous is the Antinomian School. Believing that the Creator God, Jehovah, was evil, they set out to disrupt all things connected to the Jewish God, including his laws. It was considered their duty to break any law of morality, diet, or conduct given by the Jewish God, who they considered the evil Creator God. The leader of the sect was called Nicolaites. The sect existed in Apostolic times and is mentioned in the Bible.

Revelation 2 (King James Version)
5 Remember therefore from whence thou art fallen, and repent, and do the first works; or else I will come unto thee quickly, and will remove thy candlestick out of his place, except thou repent.
6 But this thou hast, that thou hatest the deeds of the Nicolaitanes, which I also hate.

Revelation 2 (King James Version)

14 But I have a few things against thee, because thou hast there them that hold the doctrine of Balaam, who taught Balac to cast a stumbling block before the children of Israel, to eat things sacrificed unto idols, and to commit fornication.

15 So hast thou also them that hold the doctrine of the Nicolaitanes, which thing I hate.

16 Repent; or else I will come unto thee quickly, and will fight against them with the sword of my mouth.

One of the leaders of the Nocolaitanes, according to Origen, was Carpocrates, whom Tertullian called a magician and a fornicator.

Carpocretes taught that one could only escape the cosmic powers by discharging one's obligations to them and disregarding their laws. The Christian church fathers, St. Justin, Irenaeus, and Eusebius wrote that the reputation of these men (the Nicolaitanes), brought infamy upon the whole race of Christians.

Although Gnostic sects varied, they had certain points in common. These commonalities included salvation through special knowledge, and the fact that the world was corrupt, since it was created by an evil God.

According to Gnostic theology, nothing can come from the material world that is not flawed. Because of this, Gnostics did not believe that Christ could have been a corporeal being. Thus, there must be some separation or distinction between Jesus, as a man, and Christ, as a spiritual being born from the Supreme, unrevealed, and eternal God.

To closer examine this theology, we turn to Valentinus, the driving force of early Gnosticism, for an explanation. Valentinus divided Jesus Christ into two very distinct parts; Jesus, the man, and Christ, the anointed spiritual messenger of God. These two forces met in the moment of Baptism when the Spirit of God came to rest on Jesus and the Christ power entered his body.

Here Gnosticism runs aground on its own theology, for if the spiritual cannot mingle with the material then how can the Christ spirit inhabit a body? The result of the dichotomy was a schism within Gnosticism. Some held to the belief that the specter of Jesus was simply an illusion produced by Christ himself to enable him to do his work on earth. It was not real, not matter, not corporeal, and did not actually exist as a physical body would. Others came to believe that Jesus must have been a specially prepared vessel and was the perfect human body formed by the very essence of the plumora (heaven). It was this path of thought that allowed Jesus to continue as human, lover, and father.

Jesus, the man, became a vessel containing the Light of God, called Christ. In the Gnostic view we all could and should become Christs carrying the Truth and Light of God. We are all potential vehicles of the same Spirit that Jesus held within him when he was awakened to the Truth.

The suffering and death of Jesus then took on much less importance in the Gnostic view, as Jesus was simply part of the corrupt world and was suffering the indignities of this world as any man would.

The Gnostic texts seem to divide man into parts, although at times the divisions are somewhat unclear. The divisions alluded to may include the soul, which is the will of man; the spirit, which is depicted as wind or air (pneuma) and contains the holy spark that is the spirit of God in man; and the material human form, the body. The mind of man sits as a mediator between the soul, or will, and the spirit, which is connected to God.

Without the light of the truth, the spirit is held captive by the Demiurge, which enslaves man. This entrapment is called "sickness." It is this sickness that the Light came to heal and then to set us free. The third part of man, his material form, was considered a weight, an anchor, and a hindrance, keeping man attached to the corrupted earthly realm. The Demiurge proclaimed himself to be God under three separate titles:

"Now the archon (ruler) who is weak has three names. The first name is Yaltabaoth, the second is Saklas ("fool"), and the third is Samael. And he is impious in his arrogance which is in him. For he said, 'I am God and there is no other God beside me,' for he is ignorant of his strength, the place from which he had come." Apocryphon of John

As we read the text, we must realize that Gnosticism conflicted with traditional Christianity. Overall, theology can rise and fall upon small words and terms. If Jesus was not God, his death and thus his atonement meant nothing. His suffering meant nothing. Even the resurrection meant nothing, if one's view of Jesus was that he was not human to begin with, as was true with some Gnostics.

For the Gnostics, resurrection of the dead was unthinkable since flesh as well as all matter are destined to perish. According to Gnostic theology, there was no resurrection of the flesh, but only of the soul. How the soul would be resurrected was explained differently by various

Gnostic groups, but all denied the resurrection of the body. To the enlightened Gnostic the actual person was the spirit who used the body as an instrument to survive in the material world but did not identify with it.

> *29. Jesus said: If the flesh came into being because of spirit, it is a marvel, but if spirit came into being because of the body, it would be a marvel of marvels. I marvel indeed at how great wealth has taken up residence in this poverty.*
>
> > *Gospel of Thomas*

Owing to the Gnostic belief of such a separation of spirit and body, it was thought that the Christ spirit within the body of Jesus departed the body before the crucifixion. Others said the body was an illusion and the crucifixion was a sham perpetrated by an eternal spirit on the men that sought to kill it. Lastly, some suggested that Jesus deceived the soldiers into thinking he was dead. The resurrection under this circumstance became a lie, which allowed Jesus to escape and live on in anonymity, hiding, living as a married man, and raising a family until his natural death.

Think of the implications to the orthodox Christian world if the spirit of God departed from Jesus as it fled and laughed as the body was crucified. This is the implication of the Gnostic interpretation of the death of Jesus when he cries out, "My power, my power, why have you left me?" as the Christ spirit left his body before his death. What are the ramifications to the modern Christian if the Creator God, the Demiurge, is more evil than his creation? Can a creation rise above its creator? Is it possible for man to find the spark within himself that calls to the Supreme God and free himself of his evil creator?

Although, in time, the creation myth and other Gnostic differences began to be swept under the rug, it was the division between Jesus and the Christ spirit that put them at odds with the emerging orthodox church. At the establishment of the doctrine of the trinity, the mainline church firmly set a divide between themselves and the Gnostics.

To this day there is a battle raging in the Christian world as believers and seekers attempt to reconcile today's Christianity to the sect of the early Christian church called, "Gnosticism."

The History of the Gospel of Judas

The newly discovered Gospel of Judas is very controversial for several reasons. Theologically, it is divisive due to its Gnostic theology. The main controversy in the text revolves around the theory that Jesus asked Judas to betray Him in order to fulfill His destiny and the scriptures. If this is true it would make Judas a saint and not the sinner and traitor as believed by the mainline church.

The text is also interesting simply because it is written in Coptic. Documents from the time period and region where the Coptic language was native are a rare find.

The word Coptic is an Arabic corruption of the Greek word Aigyptos, which in turn comes from the word Hikaptah, one of the names of the city of Memphis, the first capital of ancient Egypt.

There has never been a Coptic state or government per se, however, the word has been used to generally define a culture and language present in the area of Egypt within a particular timeframe.

The known history of the Copts starts with King Mina the first King, who united the northern and southern kingdoms of Egypt circa 3050 B.C. The ancient Egyptian civilization under the rule of the Pharaohs lasted over 3000 years. Saint Mina (named after the king) is one of the major Coptic saints. He was martyred in 309 A.D.

The culture has come to be recognized as one containing distinctive language, art, architecture, and even certain religious systems. There is even a very distinctive Coptic Christian church system with its own canon, which contains several more books than those of the Protestant or Catholic Bibles.

The religious controversy of the Gospel of Judas is compelling, if for no other reason than that of its differing view, which forces us to re-examine the way we read and understand the place, path, and actions of Judas and his act of betrayal.

The Gospels and the Book of Acts tell the story of Judas' betrayal of Jesus and the end to which Judas came. The canonical books refer to Judas as a traitor, betrayer, and as one influenced by the devil. However, the Gospel of Judas turns this idea on its head by claiming the Judas was requested, if not required, to plan and carry out the treachery that would be the impetus for the crucifixion. The plan was to surrender Jesus to the authorities so that scripture and prophecy could be fulfilled, and Jesus was the person devising the plan.

Most scholars agree that the Gospels of Matthew, Mark, Luke, and John were written between the date of Jesus' death and about 90 A.D. The Gospel of Judas was written originally in Greek around A.D. 180 at the earliest.

If this is true, Judas could not have been the author. For Judas to have penned this work he would have been about 120 years of age at the time of its writing. Discounting this possibility, the original author is unknown.

Dates of the original texts are based on words and usage common to certain periods of time. This is comparable to how slang and catch phrases pass in and out of vogue in our own language.

Another way of narrowing down the date of the original text is to look for references to it in other writings. This would set the date marking the latest the text could have been written.

Tixeront, translated by Raemers, states: "Besides these Gospels, we know that there once existed a Gospel of Bartholomew, a Gospel of Thaddeus, mentioned in the decree of Pope Gelasius, and a Gospel of Judas Iscariot in use among the Cainites and spoken of by St. Irenaeus."

In Roberts-Donaldson's translation from Irenaeus the church father states, "Others again declare that Cain derived his being from the Power above, and acknowledge that Esau, Korah, the Sodomites, and all such persons, are related to themselves. On this account, they add, they have been assailed by the Creator, yet no one of them has suffered injury. For Sophia was in the habit of carrying off that which belonged to her from them to herself. They declare that Judas the traitor was thoroughly acquainted with these things, and that he alone, knowing the truth as no others did, accomplished the mystery of the betrayal; by him all things, both earthly and heavenly, were thus thrown into confusion. They produce a fictitious history of this kind, which they style the Gospel of Judas."

Irenaeus went on to say that the writings came from what he called a "Cainite" Gnostic sect that jousted with orthodox Christianity. He also accused the Cainites of lauding the biblical murderer Cain, the Sodomites and Judas, whom they regarded as the keeper of secret mysteries.

Knowing the dates of the writings of Irenaeus further clarifies the date to be around or before 180 A.D. Of course, this affects the Gospel of Judas only if we conclude that the text Irenaeus spoke of is the same text we have today. Sadly, there is no way to know with any certainty, but we do have a few clues.

Cain is not mentioned in the version of the Gospel of Judas we have today. Furthermore, the evolution of cosmology tends to be from the simple to the complex and this trend is shown in the current version since Yaldabaoth, who is also called "Nebro" the "rebel", is presented as the creator of Saklas and it is Saklas who is depicted later in the Gospel of Judas as the creator mankind and the physical world. However, in other Gnostic writings, Yaldabaoth is the "demiurge" or fashioner of the world, and is clearly identified as the same deity as Saklas. This means that in the Gospel of Judas there has been a split between Yaldaboth and Saklas, leading to a more complex cosmology. This indicates that the Gospel of Judas we have today was written later than that of which Irenaeus speaks, since in his time these deities were one and the same.

Now the archon who is weak has three names. The first name is Yaltabaoth, the second is Saklas ("fool"), and the third is Samael. And he is impious in his arrogance which is in him. For he said, 'I am God and there is no other God beside me,' for he is ignorant of his strength, the place from which he had come."

Apocryphon of John, ca. 200 AD.

As for the dating of the copy found in Egypt, the formation of certain letters also change with time and the style of the lettering within the texts places the copies within a certain period. The 26-page Judas text is a copy in Coptic of the original Gospel of Judas, which was written in Greek the century before.

Radioactive-carbon-dating tests as well as experts in ancient languages have established that the copy was written between 220 and 340 A.D.

The discovered Gospel was written on papyrus, probably at a Gnostic monastery in Egypt. Although other copies may have been made they were probably lost in St. Athanasius's fourth-century campaign to destroy all heretical texts. All texts not accepted by the newly established church were to be burned. Heresy was not to be tolerated, and Gnosticism was considered at the top of the list. Not only was Gnosticism different from the orthodox theology, it condoned a personal search for God through knowledge and that was something outside the control of the church. To maintain its control, the new church had to crush these beliefs.

In order to protect the text from Athanasius's soldiers it is thought a Gnostic monk or scribe buried copies of certain Gnostic texts in an area of tombs in Egypt. These were not discovered until the late 1970s. The Gospel was one of three texts found that were bound together in a single codex.

The gospel was unearthed in 1978 by a farmer. He found a small container like a tomb box in a cave near El Minya, Egypt. In the small, carved, and sealed box was part of a codex, or collection of devotional texts.

The farmer sold the codex to an antiquities dealer in Cairo. The deal was kept secret but was reported to have taken place in 1983. The antiquities dealer was unaware of the content of the codex when he offered the gospel for sale to the Coptic studies scholar, Stephen Emmel, of Germany's University of Munster and another scholar. The meeting took place in a Geneva, Switzerland hotel room.

It was Emmel who examined the codex and first suspected the papyrus sheets discussed Judas. Although the text more than intrigued Emmel, the asking price was so high at $3 million dollars U.S. that there was no way to afford the purchase.

The seller was offered a price that was an order of magnitude lower than the asking price. This, the seller took as an insult and the deal stalled.

Due to the frustration brought about by not having his greed satisfied, the dealer stored the codex in a safe in a

Hicksville, N.Y. bank for 16 years. There, away from the dry desert air, in the box with higher humidity, it deteriorated and crumbled until Zurich-based antiquities dealer Frieda Nussberger-Tchacos purchased it in 2000 for a sum much less than the original asking price. The codex was then acquired by the Maecenas Foundation for Ancient Art in Switzerland in 2001.

The foundation invited National Geographic to help with the restoration in 2004.

Over the next 5 years thousands of pieces of papyrus were placed back together like a jigsaw puzzle. Thousands of pieces, some so small they contained only a letter or two were restored to their position in the text using tweezers and computer imaging.

Once completed, a team of scholars translated the document into English, as best they could, considering the condition of the document and the number of pieces missing. The restored original is now housed in Cairo's Coptic Museum. A rendering of the text in Coptic can be seen at:

http://www.nationalgeographic.com/lostgospel/_pdf/Cop ticGospelOfJudas.pdf

Because of the extreme age and ill-treatment of the text much of it is illegible. There are gaps and holes in the codex. Entire lines are missing. Some parts of the translation were done on a "best-guess" basis. If there were letters missing from common words of phrases the translators could assume and replace letters and even words or phrases. When the gaps became larger or the meaning of the phrase was uncertain the translators simple noted the absence of data.

In this rendering we have attempted two bold moves. We wished to present a more engaging interpretation for the public, which necessarily demanded notes and explanations available at the point the ideas were encountered. We also wished to attempt to fill in some of the gaps in the text if possible.

As a matter of a disclaimer, it should be understood that the original translators did a remarkable job with the thousands of slivers and chips of papyrus that made up the codex. Once reconstructed, it became obvious that much of the text was simply missing, having disintegrated into dust and powder, never to be read again.

The text presented here takes the work done by many others and places the Gospel of Judas into a more readable language and format along with in-line commentary. It then expands the text, filling in the gaps as best it could be done, based on an understanding of the Gnostic theology, historical information, textual references, and logical flow of conversation.

All words or phases in parentheses indicate those additions made to the text, either as a matter of filling in the missing letters, words, or lines; or as a matter of clarification of ambiguous wording in the original text or its translation. When a word could be translated in more than one way, a slash "/" was used to note the various choices.

Commentary are marked clearly as "Notes" and are place in italic font within the text.

The reader should keep the probable function of the text in mind. The title gives some hint. It is not "The Gospel According to Judas", but it is instead, "The Gospel of Judas." This indicates that the writer wanted to exalt Judas, his position and contribution according to the theology being espoused and propagated by the text.

Knowing these things, the words and lines missing in the text can be a matter of educated and reasonable assumptions. They are, however, assumptions nonetheless.

Let us look now at the Gospel of Judas.

The Gospel of Judas

This is the proclamation, which was secretly revealed to Judas Iscariot by Jesus during that eight-day period that included (that was) the three days before he (Jesus) celebrated Passover (one translator has "celebrated his passion / suffering).

Note: The proclamation is not the logos, word or Christ for the orthodox church. The word here is a proclamation of judgment as in a court verdict.

1. Jesus appeared on earth to perform miracles and wondrous acts in order to save humanity.
Because some conducted themselves in a righteous way and others continued in their sins, he decided to call the twelve disciples.

2. He began to talk to them about the mysteries that lay beyond this world and what would happen at this world's end (at the end). He often changed his appearance and was not seen as himself but looked like

a child (some translators have apparition or spirit) when he was with his disciples.

3. He came upon his disciples in Judea once when they were sitting together piously (training their piety – training in godliness). As he got closer to the disciples he saw they were sitting together, giving thanks and saying a prayer over the bread (Eucharist / thanksgiving). He laughed.

4. The disciples asked Him, "Rabbi, why are you laughing at our prayer of thanks? Have we not acted appropriately?"
He said, "I am not laughing at you. It is just that you are not doing this because you want to. You are doing this because your god (has to be / will be) praised."

5. They said, "Rabbi, you are the (earthly / only) son of our god."
Jesus answered, "How do you know me? (Do you think you know me?) I say to you truly, no one among you in this generation (in this race) will understand me."

6. His disciples heard this and became enraged and

began mumbling profanities and mocking him in their hearts. When Jesus saw their inability (to understand what he said to them (their stupidity), he said,) "Why did you get so upset that you became angry? Your god, who is inside of you, (and your own lack of understanding guides you and) have instigated this anger in your (mind / soul). (I challenge) any man among you to show me who is (understanding enough) to bring out the perfect man and stand and face me."

7. They all said, "We are strong enough."
But in their (true being) spirits none dared to stand in front of him except for Judas Iscariot. Judas was able to stand in front of him, but even he could not look Jesus in the eyes, and he turned his face away.

Note: It is uncertain as to the reason Judas did not look at Jesus. It was a custom of respect not to look a superior in the eyes. Either Judas was unable to look at Jesus or was constrained by the position of Jesus as his Rabbi.

8. Judas said to Him, "I know who you are and where you came from. You are from the everlasting (eternal) aeon (realm or kingdom) of Barbelo (Barbelo's

everlasting kingdom). I am not worthy to speak the name of the one who sent you."

9. Jesus knew that Judas was capable of understanding (showing forth / thinking about) something that was glorious, so Jesus said to him, "Walk away (step a distance away) from the others and I will tell you about the mysteries of God (the reign of God / kingdom of God).

10. It is possible for you to get there, but the path will cause you great grief because you will be replaced so that the twelve may be complete with their god again."
Judas asked him, "When will you tell me how the great day of light will dawn for this generation (race)? When will you explain these things?"
But as he asked these things, Jesus left him.

11. At the dawn of the next day after this happened, Jesus appeared to his disciples.
They asked Him, "Rabbi, where did you go and what did you do when you left us?"
Jesus said to them, "I went to another generation (race) that is a greater and holier generation (race)."

12. His disciples asked him, "Lord, what is this great race that is superior to us and holier than us, that is not now in this realm (kingdom)?"

When Jesus heard this, he laughed and said to them, "Why are you thinking in your hearts about the mighty and holy race (generation)? So be it - I will tell you. No one born in this age (realm / aeon) will see that (generation / race), and not even the multitude (army) of angels (controlling) the stars will rule over that generation (race), and no mortal (corruptible) person can associate (belong) with it.

13. That generation does not come from (a realm) which has become (mortal / corrupted). The generation of people among (you) is from the generation of humanity (of inferior / without) power, which (cannot associate with the) other powers (above) by (whom) you rule / are ruled."

When (the /his) disciples heard this, they were all troubled in (their heart / spirit). They were speechless (could not utter a word).

Note: This begins a distinction drawn between the

generation or race of mankind, which is inferior, decaying, and unenlightened, and the "great generation or race," which is enlightened, incorruptible, and eternal. There are only two races; those who have gnosis and those who do not. Interestingly, Jesus does not place the disciples in the great generation.

14. On another day Jesus came up to (them). They said to (him), "Rabbi, we have seen you in a (dream), because we all had weighty (dreams about a night you were taken away / arrested)."
(He said), "Why have (you come to me when you have) gone into hiding?"

15. They said, "There was (an imposing building with a great altar in it and twelve men, (which we would say were) the priests, and there was a name, and a crowd of people waiting (enduring because of their perseverance) at that altar, (for) the priest (to come and receive) the offerings. (However) we kept waiting (we were tenacious also)."
(Jesus asked), "What were (the priests) like?"
    They said, "Some (of them would fast) for two weeks; (others would) sacrifice their own children, others their

wives, (all the while) in praise (offered in) humility with each other; some have sex with other men; some murder; some commit a plethora of sins and acts of crime. And the men who stand in front of the altar call upon your (name / authority), and in all the acts springing from their lack of knowledge (lack of light), the sacrifices are brought to completion (by their hands) (the alter remained full through their handiwork of slaughtering the sacrifices)."

After they said these things they became uneasy and quiet.

16. Jesus asked them, "Why are you bothered? So be it, I tell you that all the priests who have stood before that altar call upon my name. I have told I you many times that my name has been written on the (judgment) of this race (and on) the stars through the human generations. In my name (these people) have planted barren trees, (and have done so) without any honor."

17. Jesus said to them, "You are like those men you have seen conducting the offerings at the altar. That is the god you serve, and the twelve men you have seen represent you. The cattle you saw that were brought for

sacrifice represent the many people you have led (will lead) astray before that altar. (You) will stand (lead / represent) and use my name in that way, as will the generations of the pious and you all will remain loyal to "him." (Some translations have- "The lord of chaos will establish his place in this way.") After "him" another man will lead from (the group of fornicators), and another (will lead at the alter from those who) murder children, and another from those who are homosexuals, and (another) those who fast, and (one will stand from) the rest of those who pollution themselves and who are lawlessness and who sin, and (from) those who say, 'We are like the angels'; they are the stars that (make everything happen / bring everything to an end).

18. It has been said to the human generations, 'Look, God has received your sacrifice from the hands of a priest.' But the priest is a minister of error (minister in error / ministers but is in sin). But it is the Lord, the Lord of all (the fullness of the divine), who commands, 'On the last day (of time) they will be shamed (some have - "at the end of days").'"

Note: Jesus tells the disciples that they are loyal to the wrong god. He goes on to say that they are the ones who murder, fornicate, and sin. Furthermore, Jesus tells them that they will lead people into a spiritual slaughter like the cattle they saw sacrificed in their dream. At this time the 12 included Judas. This, along with other such verses has led many scholars to conclude that the Gospel of Judas was not depicting Judas to be the sanctified person the original translators thought him to be.

19. Jesus (told them), "Stop (sacrificing that which) you have (and stop hovering) over the altar. The priests are over your stars and your angels. They have already come to their end there. So let them (be entrapped / quarrel / fight) before you, and leave them alone. (Do not be tainted by this generation but instead eat the food of knowledge given to you by the great one.)

Note: We will see "stars" referred to often in the text. They are used to symbolize two unique concepts. It was thought that in the creation of the cosmos, luminaries were created which were powers controlling each person's destiny. It was also thought that each person was assigned a star as his or her eternal home or resting place. A good person would ascend to his or her own star to rule and rest. Thus, stars were conscious powers, carrying out orders from God, and also were places of destiny for those who escape the material plane.

20. A baker cannot feed all creation under (heaven). And (they will not give) to them (a food) and (give) to (those of the great generation the same food).

Jesus said to them, "Stop struggling with (against) me. Each of you has his own star, and every (Lines are missing here. Text could read " person has his own destiny." Or possibly, "person who does well will dwell and rest on their star").

(All things happen in their own season and all seasons are appointed. And in (the season) which has come (it is spring) for the tree (of paradise) of this aeon / age (and it will produce) for a time (then wither) but he has come to water God's paradise, and (also water this generation) that will last, because (he) will not corrupt / detour) the (path of life for) that generation, but (will guide it) from eternity to eternity."

21. Judas asked him, "Rabbi, what kind of fruit does this generation produce?"

Jesus answered, "The souls of every human generation

will die. However, when these people (of this kingdom) have completed the time in the kingdom and the living breath leaves them, their bodies will die but their souls will continue to be alive, and they will ascended (be lifted up / be taken up)."

Judas asked, "What will the remainder of the human generations do?"

Jesus said, "It is not possible to plant seeds in (rocky soil) and harvest its fruit. (This is also the way (of) the (corrupted) race (generation), (the children of this kingdom) and corruptible Sophia / wisdom) (is / are) not the hand that has created mortal people, so that their souls ascend to the eternal realms above. Amen, I say, (that no) angel (or / of) power will be able to see that (kingdom of) these to whom (belong that) holy generations (above)."

After Jesus said this, he departed.

22. Judas said, "Rabbi, you have listened to all of those others, so now listen to me too. I have seen a great vision."

23. When Jesus heard this, he laughed and said to him, "You (are the) thirteenth spirit (daemon), why are you

trying so hard / why do you excite yourself like this? However, speak up, and I will be patient with you."

Judas said to him, "In the vision I saw myself and the twelve disciples were stoning me and persecuting me very badly / severely / strongly. And I (was following you and I) arrived at a place where I saw (a large house in front me), and my eyes could not (take in / comprehend) its size. Many people were surrounding it, and the house had a roof of plants (grass / green vegetation), and in the middle of the house (there was a crowd) (and I was there with you), saying, 'Rabbi, take me in (the house) along with these people.'"

24. He responded and said, "Judas, your star has misled you. No person of mortal birth is worthy to enter the house you have seen. It is a place reserved for the saints. Not even the sun or the moon or day (light) will rule there. Only the saints will live there, in the eternal kingdom with the holy angels, always (some have the text as – "will be firmly established with the holy angels forever"). Look, I have explained to you the mysteries of the kingdom and I have taught you about the error of the stars; and (I have) sent it (on its path) on the twelve ages (aeons)."

Note: The Lost Book of Enoch tells of stars, which are the guiding forces of man and nature, erring. They become misplaced and out of order. They had to be placed or directed back into their proper paths. See The Lost Book of Enoch, by Joseph Lumpkin.

Note: There are 12 Astrological Ages. The 12 signs of the zodiac make up a 360-degree ecliptic path around the Earth, and takes 25,920 years to make the Precession of the Equinoxes. Each sign is comprised of 30 degrees of celestial longitude. Each degree of the precession is equal to 72 Earth years, and each year is equal to 50 seconds of degrees of arc of celestial longitude. In a 24 hour Earth day, the Earth rotates the entire 360 degrees of the ecliptic, allowing a person to see all 12 signs.

25. Judas said, "Rabbi, could it be that my (spiritual) seed will conquer the rulers of cosmic power (could also be rendered: "is under the control of the archons or rulers of cosmic power"?)"

26. Jesus answered and said to him, "Come (with me so)

that I (may show you the kingdom you will receive. I will show you what is to come of you and this generation), but you will be grieved when you see the kingdom and all its race (of people)."

When Judas heard Him he said to him, "What good is it if I have received it seeing that you have set me apart from that race?"

Jesus answered him and said, "You will become the thirteenth, and you will be cursed by the other generations, and you will come to rule over them. In the last days they will curse your ascent to the holy (race / kingdom)."

Note: I have chosen the word, "daemon" and not "demon" because the meaning of the text is unclear. A daemon is a divinity or supernatural being of a nature between gods and humans. In verse 24 Jesus tells Judas that he will never be worthy to enter the house, which symbolizes the eternal kingdom. Later in verse 26 Jesus seems to indicate that Judas will be cursed by the other disciples but will be raised to enter the holy generation in the last days. It is possible the interim time will be spent in what the Bible calls, "his own place."

27. Jesus said, "(Follow / come with me), so that I may teach you the (secrets) that no person (has) ever seen.

Note: This begins a creation myth based on certain Sethian Gnostic cosmology. The telling of the story appears to be an attempt to link the Gnostic cosmology to the teachings of Jesus in order to add validity and authority to the creation story and entities as well as assisting in the propagation of the sect.

There is a great and limitless kingdom, whose scope no generation of angels has seen (and in it) The Great Invisible (Spirit) is, and no angel's eye has ever seen, no thought of the heart (mind) has ever understood it, and no name can be assigned it (it cannot be named).

28. "And a brightly glowing cloud appeared there. The Great Spirit said, 'Let an angel come into being as my assistant (attendant / helper).'
"A great angel, the enlightened, divine, Self-Generated (Self-Created) one emerged from the cloud. Because of him, four other angelic lights (luminaries), (Harmozel, Oroiael, Daveithai, and Eleleth) began to exist from another cloud, and they became assistants (helpers /

attendants) to the Self-Generated angel (messenger). The Self-Created one proclaimed, 'Let (there) come into being (a star / Adam),' and it (he) came into being (at once). He (created) the first star (luminary / bright, shining being) to reign over him.

Note: Here we have a garbled text, the translation of which can go one of two ways. The words missing in the middle of the text could be Adam, who is also known as Adamas, or it could refer to a star, since the next reference is to a luminary. The direction of the text is unclear except that it is agreed that the word "it" is used in the text.

He said, 'Let angels (messengers) begin existence to adore (worship) (him),' and an innumerable plethora became existent. He said, '(Let there be) an aeon of light,' and he began existence. He created the second star to rule over him, to render service together with the innumerable plethora of angels. That is how he created the rest of the aeons of light. He made them rulers over them, and he created for them an innumerable plethora of angels to assist them.

29. "Adamas (Adam) was in the first luminous cloud

83

(the initial divine expression) that no angel has ever seen, including all those called 'God.' He (was the one) that (created the enlightened aeon and beheld) the image and produced him after the likeness of (this) angel. He made the incorruptible (generation) of Seth appear (from) the twelve (aeons and) the twenty-four (stars / angelic lights / luminaries). He made seventy-two angelic lights appear in the imperishable generation, as the will of the Spirit dictated. The seventy-two angelic lights themselves made three hundred sixty angelic lights appear in the immortal race, by following the will of the Spirit, that their number should be five for each.

Note: Seth is the son of Adam and was considered to be divine as Adam was divine. Seth produced "that incorruptible generation." He was thought to have received the knowledge that would bring freedom from the material realm, and thus, salvation.

30. "The twelve realms (aeons) of the twelve angelic lights make up / appoint their Father, with six heavens for each aeon, so that there are seventy-two heavens for the seventy-two angelic lights, and for each (there are five) skies, (producing all) three hundred sixty (skies for

the stars). They were given authority and a innumerable host of angels, for glory and adoration (worship), (and then he gave the) virgin (pure spirits), for glory and worship of all the aeons and the heavens and their firmaments (skies).

Note: The numbers assigned to the various aeons, angels, and stars have significance in both biblical number symbolism and Pythagorean numerology.

One – Unity, sovereign, God, causality.

Two – Duality and / or merging.

Three - Spiritually complete, fullness, creation.

Four – Foundations, systems, order.

Five – Spirit, grace, movement.

Six - Mankind.

Seven – God, wisdom, knowledge, perfection.

Twelve   Law, rule, authority.

Thirteen – Cursed, beyond or without law.

Twenty-four – Heavenly government, elders, a system. Duality within the system.

Seventy-two – Both elements of two and seven as well as the element of completion.

Three hundred and sixty – Elements of three and six as well as the meaning of a full cycle such as a

85

yearly cycle. An end, and a new start.

31. The totality (gathering) of those immortals is called the cosmos, that is to say perdition / decay / corruption, by the Father and the seventy-two angelic lights / luminaries who are with the Self-Created one and his seventy-two aeons. In the cosmos the first human appeared with his incorruptible powers.

Note: This first human is Adamas or Adam. It should be noted that the name "Adam" can also be rendered as "Man" in Hebrew.

32. And the aeon that appeared with his generation and the aeon in whom are the cloud of knowledge and the angel, is called El.

Note: El was the name of a Semitic god who was chief among the pantheon of gods affecting nature and society. He is father of the divine family and president of the divine assembly on the 'mount of assembly', the equivalent of Hebrew har mo'ed, which became through the Greek transliteration Armageddon. In Canaanite mythology he is known as 'the Bull', symbolizing his strength and creative force. He is called 'Creator of Created Things' which is how rivers were also metaphorically thought of. In the Biblical Garden of Eden a river flowed to form the four rivers, Tigris, Euphrates, Gihon and Pishon."

El expressed the concept of ordered government, justice and creation. The Bible never stigmatizes the Canaanite worship of El, whose authority in social affairs was recognized by the Patriarchs. His consort was Asherah, the mother goddess, represented in Canaanite sanctuaries by a natural tree (Hebrew ashera) such as the tree of life.

33. (He created the) aeon, (after that) (El) said, 'Let twelve angels come into being (in order to) rule over chaos and the (cosmos / perdition).' And look, from the cloud {called Sophia} there appeared an (angel / aeon) whose face flashed with fire and whose appearance was defiled with blood. His name was Nebro, meaning "rebel." Another angel, Saklas, also came from the cloud. So Nebro created six angels—as well as Saklas— to be assistants, and these produced twelve angels in the heavens, with each one receiving a piece of the heavens.

Note: Nebro may be a female demon who mates with

Saklas; others call Nebro by the name "Yaldaboth (child of chaos) Yaldaboth and Saklas are both names given to the insane or deficient deity that created the physical world. Also the reading could be influenced by the fact that in some mythologies Nebro is a head demon and Saklas is a head angel. Nebro has the same meaning as Nimrod, which is "rebel."

The Jews and Greeks of the day were literalists. Each and every word of the scriptures was taken at face value. Therefore, the god who created Adam and Eve was a limited and tangible god. He walked and talked and asked questions, the answers to which he did not seem to know. By building a creation story that includes Saklas the problems were solved. Now the references to multiple gods were answered and when god said let "us" create man, the references could be to Saklas and his helpers. Since the Saklas deity was limited and restricted it left the Supreme God to be "God."

34. "The twelve rulers (aeons) spoke with the twelve angels: 'Let each of you (receive a portion) and let them (that are in this) generation (be ruled by these) angels':

The first is Seth, who is called Christ.

The (second) is Harmathoth, who is (head ruler of the underworld).

The (third) is Galila.

The fourth is Yobel.

The fifth (is) Adonaios.

These are the five who ruled all of the underworld, and primarily over chaos.

Note: These five names are probably associated with the five planets known at the time the Gospel of Judas was written. They were placed on their paths and courses to keep order and give light, both real and spiritual.

35. "Then Saklas said to his angels, 'Let us create a human being in the similitude and after the figure / image / representation (of the Supreme God) .' They fashioned Adam and his wife Eve, who is called Zoe / life when she was still in the cloud.

Note: Zoe is another name for Eve in the Septuagint.

36. For it is this name (life) that all the generations seek the man, and each of them calls the woman by these names. Now, Sakla did not command (as he was

instructed) but (he commanded) the generations (of man to live so long / for a defined period of time), (but he did created them in his (Saklas') likeness). And the (ruler Saklas) said to Adam, 'You shall live long, with your children.'"

37. Judas said to Jesus, "(What length) is the long span of time that humans will live?"
Jesus said, "Why are you curious about this? Adam and his generation has lived his lifespan in the place where he received his kingdom, with his longevity bestowed by his ruler (as numbered with his ruler)."

38. Judas said to Jesus, "Does the human spirit die?"
Jesus said, "This is why God (the god of this realm) ordered Michael to loan spirits to people so that they would serve (be in servitude), but the Great One commanded Gabriel to give spirits to the great generation (race) which had no ruler over it (a generation that cannot be dominated). He gave the spirit and the soul. Therefore, the (remainder / mountain) of souls (loaned will come back to the god of this realm in the end).

Note: This passage indicates two lines of creation. For those people created by the god of this world the angel Michael was commanded to temporarily assign souls to his creation. To keep their souls they were enslaved to worship the god of this world. In contrast, the Great One commanded Gabriel to give souls to those of the great generation for eternity.

39. "(There was no) light (in this world to shine) around (the people to) allow (the) spirit (which is) within you all to dwell in this (body) among the generations of angels. But God caused knowledge to be (given) to Adam and those with him, so that the kings of chaos and the underworld might not oppress them with it."

Note: The word rendered as "rule" by most translators has the connotation of oppression.

40. Judas said to Jesus, "So what will those generations do?"
Jesus said, "Truthfully, I tell you all, that for all of them the stars bring matters to completion (heavenly apocalypse). When Saklas completes the span of time assigned for him, their first star will appear with the

generations, and they will finish what they said they would do. Then they will (have illicit sex in my name and kill (sacrifice) their children and they will fast, and they will kill their wives in praise offered in humility with each other; some have sex with other men; some will murder, some commit a plethora of sins and acts of crime all in my name, and Saklas will destroy) your star over the thirteenth aeon."

41. After that Jesus (laughed).

Note: Jesus seems to find humor in the misguided judgments or concepts of the disciples. He laughs, as if shaking his head in disbelief of the error, then attempts to give insight and correction.

(Judas asked), "Rabbi, (why do you laugh at us)?"
(He) answered (Judas and said), "I am not laughing (because of you) but at the error of the stars, because these six stars wander about with these five warriors and they all will be destroyed along with their creations."

Note: The six stars were those who, along with Saklas or

yaldaboth, created man and the cosmos. The five warriors refer to the five known planets at the time of the writing of the text. These planets were also connected with pagan worship and deities.

42. Judas said to Jesus, "Look at what those who have been baptized in your name do?"
Jesus said, "Truthfully I tell (you), this baptism done in my name (are done by those who do not know me. They sacrifice in vain to the god of this world. I baptized no one, for those baptized here have their hope here and those who follow me need no baptism for they will come) to me. In truth (I) tell you, Judas, (those offering) sacrifices to Saklas (do not offer sacrifice to the Great) God (but instead worship) everything that is evil.
"But you will exceed all of them. For you will sacrifice the man (the body that clothes / bares / contains me).

Note: Gnostic theology sets up a duality between the material world and the spiritual world. Since the god that created the material world was flawed, cruel, and insane, anything produced in that environment must be corrupted and opposed to the spiritual world. In this belief system the killing of Jesus' body was a good thing since it would free his spirit and unite it with the "Great One." Looked at from this angle, Judas was assisting Jesus in showing mankind the way. This line of reasoning must be taken as metaphorical. Some authors have suggested that Jesus had become entombed in his body and was asking Judas to free him. This cannot be so since Jesus comes and goes from the Holy Race or Generation above at will. Neither is Jesus touting mass suicide. Gnostic lived long lives and propagated their faith. The message here is that to remain detached from the material or corporeal and to strive to receive the knowledge here will free you in the life to come.

Already your horn has been raised, your anger has been ignited, your star has shown brightly, and your heart has (prevailed / been made strong / pure).

Note: The symbol horn is a phallic symbol but also a symbol of strength in much the way a rhino's horn is a sign of power and might.

Note: Although the lines added to the first half of this verse are tenuous, the information that is available establishes Judas' place according to this story. It does, however, open some questions. What was Judas' anger directed against?

Was he sacrificing Jesus because he was angry at the established religion of the day? Was it this anger that made his heart strong or pure? Was anger his motivating force? If so, it harmonizes well with certain readings of the canonical gospels, which may indicate Judas wanted to expedite Jesus' kingdom so he would have a place of authority therein.

43. "Truly (I tell you,) your last (act will become that which will free this race but it will) grieve (you and will anger this generation and) the ruler, since he will be destroyed. (And then the) image of the great race of Adam will be raised high, for before heaven, earth, and the angels, that race from the eternal realms, exists (existed). Look, you have been told everything. Lift up your eyes and look to the cloud and the light within it and the stars around it. The star that leads the way is your star (you are the star)."

44. Then, Judas raised his eyes and saw the radiant cloud, and entered it. Those standing below him heard a voice coming from the cloud, saying, (The return of the) great race (is at hand and the image of the Great One will be established in them because of Judas' sacrifice).

Note: This is the same cloud mentioned in verse 24. By entering the cloud Judas became one with the primal causality or "Great One / Supreme God." The Gnosis was imparted to him and he knew the mysteries. He then had understanding and strength to do what he was asked to do. This amounts to a transfiguration for Judas, much like that of Jesus. In the same manner, a voice from heaven announced his destiny.

45. (But the scribes waited for Judas, hoping to place a price on the head of Jesus.) Their high priests whispered that he had gone into the guest room for his prayer. But some scribes were there watching closely in order to arrest Jesus during the prayer, for they were afraid of the people, since he was accepted by everyone as a prophet. They approached Judas and said to him, "Why are you here? You are Jesus' disciple." Judas answered them in the way they wished. And he was given an amount of money and he handed Jesus over to them.

Note: We read of Judas' entrance into the radiant cloud and then his transaction with the scribes but there is no transition. It is possible the cloud is a metaphor for divine knowledge of the primal causality or Great God that produced Barbelo. See verse 28.

Note: The actual betrayal of Jesus by Judas is drastically downplayed. Only one paragraph is devoted to the actual act. Within this single paragraph no details are offered.

The gospel is constructed to give the reason for the betrayal. Building the rational of the act becomes far more important than the act itself, given the fact that it was the body that clothed Jesus that was destroyed and not the inner spirit. Shedding the body fulfilled destiny and freed the Christ spirit.

This was done as a demonstration of Jesus' belief in the immortal and eternal realm, which lay beyond human senses. The lesson of the Gospel of Judas and of Gnosticism in general had to do with reaching inside to gain knowledge of the unseen spiritual world. The orthodox church taught that only through martyrdom or the blessing of the church could one pass into the spiritual realm. Jesus was teaching another way. His death was the only way to exemplify his faith and show his disciples there was more than they could see in the material world. According to the Gnostic texts, the death of Jesus did not bring salvation. His life and death taught and provided knowledge, that if understood, would free the human race of its chains and allow it to ascend to the immortal realm.

This ends the Gospel of Judas.

Who Was Judas?

Judas was the son of Simon Iscariot (John 6:71, 13:2). He was a Jew from the tribe of Benjamin. (Gal 1:13-14, Phil. 3:5) The area of his birth is now called the occupied West Bank.

Out of the twelve men chosen by Jesus, Judas Iscariot was the only one born outside of Galilee. Judas was from Judea. The name, Iscariot may indicate that he was born in Cerioth (Kerrioth), a city of Judea, although others argue that a copyist error transposed two letters making Judas' named to be "Sicariot," a member of the party of the Sicarii. This comes from the Greek word for "assassins" and was a group of fanatical nationalists who sought to overthrow Roman by means of terrorism and murder. Judas Iscariot could have meant Judas the assasin.

In attempting to clarify the name one must ask if it is reasonable to expect the father and son to both be terrorists and zealots. It is far more likely the name would be derived from the city and not a factional political movement.

The book of Joshua mentions such a town in Joshua 15:25. As linguistic studies continue, it has been suggested that the word may simply mean, "town" as render in the same verse of the Revised Standard Version.

Judas was the one who kept the funds for Jesus and the disciples. At this time they seemed to have lived a rather communistic existence and share a common treasury. Judas was the treasurer (John 12:4-6)

Among the more liberal theologians who question the historicity of the gospels there is a general belief that the Bible should interpreted metaphorically. In this view of biblical interpretation Judas may not have existed as a person at all, but rather was a personification of an entire people. Judas comes from the name Judah, which means "praise." The name is a cognate of Judea, the tribe that came to symbolize and lend its name to the entire nation of the Jews. One theory holds that Judas was a personification of the Jews and a metaphor for the Jews and their rejection and betrayal of Jesus.

So, who was this man who became synonymous with greed and betrayal?

First, we will present the biblical information as recorded in the New Testament in the gospels of Matthew, Mark, Luke, and John as well as the book of Acts. We will then discern what information is contained and implied from the Bible text. We will then compare and contrast the information in the gospel of Judas to that found in the Bible.

First Impressions In The Scriptures

First impressions mean a lot. Let us look at the first time Judas is mentioned in each of the Gospels.

Matthew 10

1 And when he had called unto him his twelve disciples, he gave them power against unclean spirits, to cast them out, and to heal all manner of sickness and all manner of disease.

2 Now the names of the twelve apostles are these; The first, Simon, who is called Peter, and Andrew his brother; James the son of Zebedee, and John his brother;

3 Philip, and Bartholomew; Thomas, and Matthew the publican; James the son of Alphaeus, and Lebbaeus, whose surname was Thaddaeus;

4 Simon the Canaanite, and Judas Iscariot, who also betrayed him.

5 These twelve Jesus sent forth, and commanded them, saying, Go not into the way of the Gentiles, and into any city of the Samaritans enter ye not:

6 But go rather to the lost sheep of the house of Israel.

Mark 3

1 And he entered again into the synagogue; and there was a man there which had a withered hand.

2 And they watched him, whether he would heal him on the sabbath day; that they might accuse him.

3 And he saith unto the man which had the withered hand, Stand forth.

4 And he saith unto them, Is it lawful to do good on the sabbath days, or to do evil? to save life, or to kill? But they held their peace.

5 And when he had looked round about on them with anger, being grieved for the hardness of their hearts, he saith unto the man, Stretch forth thine hand. And he stretched it out: and his hand was restored whole as the other.

6 And the Pharisees went forth, and straightway took counsel with the Herodians against him, how they might destroy him.

7 But Jesus withdrew himself with his disciples to the sea: and a great multitude from Galilee followed him, and from Judaea,

8 And from Jerusalem, and from Idumaea, and from beyond Jordan; and they about Tyre and Sidon, a great

multitude, when they had heard what great things he did, came unto him.

9 And he spake to his disciples, that a small ship should wait on him because of the multitude, lest they should throng him.

10 For he had healed many; insomuch that they pressed upon him for to touch him, as many as had plagues.

11 And unclean spirits, when they saw him, fell down before him, and cried, saying, Thou art the Son of God.

12 And he straitly charged them that they should not make him known.

13 And he goeth up into a mountain, and calleth unto him whom he would: and they came unto him.

14 And he ordained twelve, that they should be with him, and that he might send them forth to preach,

15 And to have power to heal sicknesses, and to cast out devils:

16 And Simon he surnamed Peter;

17 And James the son of Zebedee, and John the brother of James; and he surnamed them Boanerges, which is, The sons of thunder:

18 And Andrew, and Philip, and Bartholomew, and Matthew, and Thomas, and James the son of Alphaeus,

and Thaddaeus, and Simon the Canaanite,

19 And Judas Iscariot, which also betrayed him: and they went into an house.

Luke 6

1 And it came to pass on the second sabbath after the first, that he went through the corn fields; and his disciples plucked the ears of corn, and did eat, rubbing them in their hands.

2 And certain of the Pharisees said unto them, Why do ye that which is not lawful to do on the sabbath days?

3 And Jesus answering them said, Have ye not read so much as this, what David did, when himself was an hungred, and they which were with him;

4 How he went into the house of God, and did take and eat the shewbread, and gave also to them that were with him; which it is not lawful to eat but for the priests alone?

5 And he said unto them, That the Son of man is Lord also of the sabbath.

6 And it came to pass also on another sabbath, that he entered into the synagogue and taught: and there was a man whose right hand was withered.

7 And the scribes and Pharisees watched him,

whether he would heal on the sabbath day; that they might find an accusation against him.

8 But he knew their thoughts, and said to the man which had the withered hand, Rise up, and stand forth in the midst. And he arose and stood forth.

9 Then said Jesus unto them, I will ask you one thing; Is it lawful on the sabbath days to do good, or to do evil? to save life, or to destroy it?

10 And looking round about upon them all, he said unto the man, Stretch forth thy hand. And he did so: and his hand was restored whole as the other.

11 And they were filled with madness; and communed one with another what they might do to Jesus.

12 And it came to pass in those days, that he went out into a mountain to pray, and continued all night in prayer to God.

13 And when it was day, he called unto him his disciples: and of them he chose twelve, whom also he named apostles;

14 Simon, (whom he also named Peter,) and Andrew his brother, James and John, Philip and Bartholomew,

15 Matthew and Thomas, James the son of Alphaeus, and Simon called Zelotes,

16 And Judas the brother of James, and Judas

Iscariot, which also was the traitor.

John 6

38 For I came down from heaven, not to do mine own will, but the will of him that sent me.

39 And this is the Father's will which hath sent me, that of all which he hath given me I should lose nothing, but should raise it up again at the last day.

40 And this is the will of him that sent me, that every one which seeth the Son, and believeth on him, may have everlasting life: and I will raise him up at the last day.

41 The Jews then murmured at him, because he said, I am the bread which came down from heaven.

42 And they said, Is not this Jesus, the son of Joseph, whose father and mother we know? how is it then that he saith, I came down from heaven?

43 Jesus therefore answered and said unto them, Murmur not among yourselves.

44 No man can come to me, except the Father which hath sent me draw him: and I will raise him up at the last day.

45 It is written in the prophets, And they shall be all taught of God. Every man therefore that hath heard, and hath learned of the Father, cometh unto me.

46 Not that any man hath seen the Father, save he which is of God, he hath seen the Father.

47 Verily, verily, I say unto you, He that believeth on me hath everlasting life.

48 I am that bread of life.

49 Your fathers did eat manna in the wilderness, and are dead.

50 This is the bread which cometh down from heaven, that a man may eat thereof, and not die.

51 I am the living bread which came down from heaven: if any man eat of this bread, he shall live for ever: and the bread that I will give is my flesh, which I will give for the life of the world.

52 The Jews therefore strove among themselves, saying, How can this man give us his flesh to eat?

53 Then Jesus said unto them, Verily, verily, I say unto you, Except ye eat the flesh of the Son of man, and drink his blood, ye have no life in you.

54 Whoso eateth my flesh, and drinketh my blood, hath eternal life; and I will raise him up at the last day.

55 For my flesh is meat indeed, and my blood is drink indeed.

56 He that eateth my flesh, and drinketh my blood, dwelleth in me, and I in him.

57 As the living Father hath sent me, and I live by the Father: so he that eateth me, even he shall live by me.

58 This is that bread which came down from heaven: not as your fathers did eat manna, and are dead: he that eateth of this bread shall live for ever.

59 These things said he in the synagogue, as he taught in Capernaum.

60 Many therefore of his disciples, when they had heard this, said, This is an hard saying; who can hear it?

61 When Jesus knew in himself that his disciples murmured at it, he said unto them, Doth this offend you?

62 What and if ye shall see the Son of man ascend up where he was before?

63 It is the spirit that quickeneth; the flesh profiteth nothing: the words that I speak unto you, they are spirit, and they are life.

64 But there are some of you that believe not. For Jesus knew from the beginning who they were that believed not, and who should betray him.

65 And he said, Therefore said I unto you, that no man can come unto me, except it were given unto him of my Father.

66 From that time many of his disciples went back,

and walked no more with him.

67 Then said Jesus unto the twelve, Will ye also go away?

68 Then Simon Peter answered him, Lord, to whom shall we go? thou hast the words of eternal life.

69 And we believe and are sure that thou art that Christ, the Son of the living God.

70 Jesus answered them, Have not I chosen you twelve, and one of you is a devil?

71 He spake of Judas Iscariot the son of Simon: for he it was that should betray him, being one of the twelve.

In each incident the first time, and indeed, every time the name Judas is mentioned he is labeled as the one who betrayed Jesus. Judas is clearly and repeated marked as a traitor. This sets the mood for the entire panoply of scenes and verses regarding Judas. The story in each gospel builds on these first lines.

The Biblical Account of Judas

Now, let us look at the entire Biblical account of Judas. Information gleaned from the biblical references will be compared and contrasted to those in the Gospel of Judas. One may think, on prima fascia, there would be complete divergence and contradiction, and there are many, but the parallels are surprising.

Matthew

Chapter 26

14: Then one of the twelve, who was called Judas Iscariot, went to the chief priests

15: and said, "What will you give me if I deliver him to you?" And they paid him thirty pieces of silver.

16: And from that moment he sought an opportunity to betray him.

17: Now on the first day of Unleavened Bread the disciples came to Jesus, saying, "Where will you have us prepare for you to eat the passover?"

18: He said, "Go into the city to a certain one, and say to him, `The Teacher says, My time is at hand; I will keep the passover at your house with my disciples.'"

19: And the disciples did as Jesus had directed them, and they prepared the passover.

20: When it was evening, he sat at table with the twelve disciples;

21: and as they were eating, he said, "Truly, I say to you, one of you will betray me."

22: And they were very sorrowful, and began to say to him one after another, "Is it I, Lord?"

23: He answered, "He who has dipped his hand in the dish with me, will betray me.

24: The Son of man goes as it is written of him, but woe to that man by whom the Son of man is betrayed! It would have been better for that man if he had not been born."

25: Judas, who betrayed him, said, "Is it I, Rabbi?" He said to him, "You have said so."

47: While he [Jesus] was still speaking, Judas came, one of the twelve, and with him a great crowd with swords and clubs, from the chief priests and the elders of the people.

48: Now the betrayer had given them a sign, saying, "The one I shall kiss is the man; seize him."

49: And he came up to Jesus at once and said, "Hail, Rabbi!" And he kissed him.

50: Jesus said to him, "Friend, why are you here?" Then they came up and laid hands on Jesus and seized him.

Chapter 27

1: When morning came, all the chief priests and the elders of the people took counsel against Jesus to put him to death;

2: and they bound him and led him away and delivered him to Pilate the governor.

3: When Judas, his betrayer, saw that he was condemned, he repented and brought back the thirty pieces of silver to the chief priests and the elders,

4: saying, "I have sinned in betraying innocent blood." They said, "What is that to us? See to it yourself."

5: And throwing down the pieces of silver in the temple, he departed; and he went and hanged himself.

6: But the chief priests, taking the pieces of silver, said, "It is not lawful to put them into the treasury, since they are blood money."

7: So they took counsel, and bought with them the potter's field, to bury strangers in.

8: Therefore that field has been called the Field of Blood to this day.

9: Then was fulfilled what had been spoken by the prophet Jeremiah, saying, "And they took the thirty pieces of silver, the price of him on whom a price had been set by some of the sons of Israel,

10: and they gave them for the potter's field, as the Lord directed me."

Mark

Chapter 14

1: It was now two days before the Passover and the feast of Unleavened Bread. And the chief priests and the scribes were seeking how to arrest him by stealth, and kill him;

2: for they said, "Not during the feast, lest there be a tumult of the people."

10: Then Judas Iscariot, who was one of the twelve, went to the chief priests in order to betray him to them.

11: And when they heard it they were glad, and promised to give him money. And he sought an opportunity to betray him.

12: And on the first day of Unleavened Bread, when they sacrificed the passover lamb, his disciples said to him, "Where will you have us go and prepare for you to eat the passover?"

13: And he sent two of his disciples, and said to them, "Go into the city, and a man carrying a jar of water will meet you; follow him,

14: and wherever he enters, say to the householder, `The Teacher says, Where is my guest room, where I am to eat the passover with my disciples?'

15: And he will show you a large upper room furnished and ready; there prepare for us." 16: And the disciples set out and went to the city, and found it as he had told them; and they prepared the passover.

17: And when it was evening he came with the twelve.

18: And as they were at table eating, Jesus said, "Truly, I say to you, one of you will betray me, one who is eating with me."

19: They began to be sorrowful, and to say to him one after another, "Is it I?"

20: He said to them, "It is one of the twelve, one who is dipping bread into the dish with me.

21: For the Son of man goes as it is written of him, but woe to that man by whom the Son of man is betrayed! It would have been better for that man if he had not been born."

43: And immediately, while he was still speaking, Judas came, one of the twelve, and with him a crowd with swords and clubs, from the chief priests and the scribes and the elders.

44: Now the betrayer had given them a sign, saying, "The one I shall kiss is the man; seize him and lead him away under guard."

45: And when he came, he went up to him at once, and said, "Rabbi!" And he kissed him.

46: And they laid hands on him and seized him.

Luke

Chapter 22

1: Now the feast of Unleavened Bread drew near, which is called the Passover.

2: And the chief priests and the scribes were seeking how to put him to death; for they feared the people.

3: Then Satan entered into Judas called Iscariot, who was of the number of the twelve;

4: he went away and conferred with the chief priests and officers how he might betray him to them.

5: And they were glad, and engaged to give him money.

6: So he agreed, and sought an opportunity to betray him to them in the absence of the multitude.

17: And he took a cup, and when he had given thanks he said, "Take this, and divide it among yourselves;

18: for I tell you that from now on I shall not drink of the fruit of the vine until the kingdom of God comes."

19: And he took bread, and when he had given thanks he broke it and gave it to them, saying, "This is my body which is given for you. Do this in remembrance of me."

20: And likewise the cup after supper, saying, "This cup which is poured out for you is the new covenant in my blood.

21: But behold the hand of him who betrays me is with me on the table.

22: For the Son of man goes as it has been determined; but woe to that man by whom he is betrayed!"

23: And they began to question one another, which of them it was that would do this.

45: And when he rose from prayer, he came to the disciples and found them sleeping for sorrow,

46: and he said to them, "Why do you sleep? Rise and pray that you may not enter into temptation."

47: While he was still speaking, there came a crowd, and the man called Judas, one of the twelve, was leading them. He drew near to Jesus to kiss him;

48: but Jesus said to him, "Judas, would you betray the Son of man with a kiss?"

John

Chapter 13

1: Now before the feast of the Passover, when Jesus knew that his hour had come to depart out of this world to the Father, having loved his own who were in the world, he loved them to the end.

2: And during supper, when the devil had already put it into the heart of Judas Iscariot, Simon's son, to betray him,

3: Jesus, knowing that the Father had given all things into his hands, and that he had come from God and was going to God,

4: rose from supper, laid aside his garments, and girded himself with a towel.

21: When Jesus had thus spoken, he was troubled in spirit, and testified, "Truly, truly, I say to you, one of you will betray me."

22: The disciples looked at one another, uncertain of whom he spoke.

23: One of his disciples, whom Jesus loved, was lying close to the breast of Jesus;

24: so Simon Peter beckoned to him and said, "Tell us who it is of whom he speaks."

25: So lying thus, close to the breast of Jesus, he said to him, "Lord, who is it?"

26: Jesus answered, "It is he to whom I shall give this morsel when I have dipped it." So when he had dipped the morsel, he gave it to Judas, the son of Simon Iscariot.

27: Then after the morsel, Satan entered into him. Jesus said to him, "What you are going to do, do quickly."

28: Now no one at the table knew why he said this to him.

29: Some thought that, because Judas had the money box, Jesus was telling him, "Buy what we need for the feast"; or, that he should give something to the poor.

30: So, after receiving the morsel, he immediately went out; and it was night.

John

Chapter 18

1: When Jesus had spoken these words, he went forth with his disciples across the Kidron valley, where there was a garden, which he and his disciples entered.

2: Now Judas, who betrayed him, also knew the place; for Jesus often met there with his disciples.

3: So Judas, procuring a band of soldiers and some officers from the chief priests and the Pharisees, went there with lanterns and torches and weapons.

4: Then Jesus, knowing all that was to befall him, came forward and said to them, "Whom do you seek?"

5: They answered him, "Jesus of Nazareth." Jesus said to them, "I am he." Judas, who betrayed him, was standing with them.

6: When he said to them, "I am he," they drew back and fell to the ground.

7: Again he asked them, "Whom do you seek?" And they said, "Jesus of Nazareth."

8: Jesus answered, "I told you that I am he; so, if you seek me, let these men go."

9: This was to fulfill the word which he had spoken, "Of those whom thou gavest me I lost not one."

Acts

Chapter 1

15 And in those days Peter stood up in the midst of the disciples, and said, (the number of names together were about an hundred and twenty,)

16 Men and brethren, this scripture must needs have been fulfilled, which the Holy Ghost by the mouth of David spake before concerning Judas, which was guide to them that took Jesus.

17 For he was numbered with us, and had obtained part of this ministry.

18 Now this man purchased a field with the reward of iniquity; and falling headlong, he burst asunder in the midst, and all his bowels gushed out.

19 And it was known unto all the dwellers at Jerusalem; insomuch as that field is called in their proper tongue, Aceldama, that is to say, The field of blood.

20 For it is written in the book of Psalms, Let his habitation be desolate, and let no man dwell therein: and his bishoprick let another take.

21 Wherefore of these men which have companied with us all the time that the Lord Jesus went in and out among us,

22 Beginning from the baptism of John, unto that same day that he was taken up from us, must one be ordained to be a witness with us of his resurrection.

23 And they appointed two, Joseph called Barsabas, who was surnamed Justus, and Matthias.

24 And they prayed, and said, Thou, Lord, which knowest the hearts of all men, shew whether of these two thou hast chosen,

25 That he may take part of this ministry and apostleship, from which Judas by transgression fell, that he might go to his own place.

26 And they gave forth their lots; and the lot fell upon Matthias; and he was numbered with the eleven apostles.

John 6

69 And we believe and are sure that thou art that Christ, the Son of the living God.

70 Jesus answered them, Have not I chosen you twelve, and one of you is a devil?

71 He spake of Judas Iscariot the son of Simon: for he it was that should betray him, being one of the twelve.

The Nature of Judas

Gospel of Judas: 23. When Jesus heard this, he laughed and said to him, "You (are the) thirteenth spirit (daemon), why are you trying so hard? However, speak up, and I will be patient with you."

John 6:70 Jesus answered them, Have not I chosen you twelve, and one of you is a devil?

71 He spake of Judas Iscariot the son of Simon: for he it was that should betray him, being one of the twelve.

On the surface these two statements may seem to harmonize. It may seem obvious that Judas was following his basic nature when he turned Jesus over to the authorities. However, the tone and context of these two, seemingly similar statements are in fact opposite.

In John's account the word used for devil is a word that means "accuser." The word, "devil" is a transliteration from the Greek and is set down into English with little alteration. In one or two cases it is translated into the "true" meaning, such as in 1 Tim. 3:11, where the wives of the deacons are forbidden to be slanderers, whereas the word elsewhere is rendered "devil."

Parkhurst, in his Greek Lexicon, tells us that diabolos, the word translated devil, is a compound of dia through, and ballo to cast, and means to dart or strike through; hence, to slander, to utter falsehood maliciously, to speak lies. "The word, "devil" is best to be read in English as The Liar, The Slanderer, or The Accuser.

Further hints are given in a group of scriptures describing the moment of decision when Judas left the Passover feast to go arrange for Jesus' arrest.

Luke

Chapter 22

1: Now the feast of Unleavened Bread drew near, which is called the Passover.

2: And the chief priests and the scribes were seeking how to put him to death; for they feared the people.

3: Then Satan entered into Judas called Iscariot, who was of the number of the twelve;

4: he went away and conferred with the chief priests and officers how he might betray him to them.

The word rendered "entered" can also be

"revealed." If Jesus thought Judas was literally a devil the text could read "Then Satan revealed himself as Judas…"

Yet, in other verses no such thought is entertained but instead Judas is portrayed as a man and even a friend.

In Mark 14:18-21 Jesus tells the disciples that a person who is eating with them will give Jesus over to be killed. He goes on to say that it would be better for him if he were never born. Jesus echoes Psalms 41:9, which foretells that his best friend with whom he ate will betray him.

In the gospel of Judas, Jesus calls Judas a spirit or daemon. This indicates the Jesus believes him to be a powerful spiritual being. In the mythology of the time daemons or spirits did the bidding of a god and were placed as mediators between man and the god they served. One may ask what god Jesus had in mind when addressing Judas in such a way. The statement may not be as positive as one would think, but it does place Judas and the others in a status outside of the human norm. Since Judas is referred to as the "thirteenth spirit" it can be assumed that there are twelve more. One could jump to the conclusion Jesus is referring to the twelve disciples. That would be the eleven left and the one chosen to replace Judas. This assumption would leave out the possibility of Judas being given status with the twelve rulers referred to in The Gospel of Judas verse 34. "The twelve rulers (aeons) spoke with the twelve angels: 'Let each of you (receive a portion) and let them (that are in this) generation (be ruled by these) angels'...

Of all the biblical statements relating to Judas, one of the most perplexing passages is the one in the book of Acts.

Acts 1: 23 And they appointed two, Joseph called Barsabas, who was surnamed Justus, and Matthias.

24 And they prayed, and said, Thou, Lord, which knowest the hearts of all men, shew whether of these two thou hast chosen,

25 That he may take part of this ministry and apostleship, from which Judas by transgression fell, that he might go to his own place.

The reader is left to wonder what and where "his own place" may be. Judas is called "a devil" and the "son of perdition" and we are told he went to "his own place" after his suicide. The only clue we are given to the mystery comes from Second Thessalonians.

2 Thessalonians 2

1 Now we beseech you, brethren, by the coming of our Lord Jesus Christ, and by our gathering together unto him,

2 That ye be not soon shaken in mind, or be troubled, neither by spirit, nor by word, nor by letter as from us, as that the day of Christ is at hand.

3 Let no man deceive you by any means: for that day shall not come, except there come a falling away first, and that man of sin be revealed, the son of perdition;

4 Who opposeth and exalteth himself above all that is called God, or that is worshipped; so that he as God sitteth in the temple of God, shewing himself that he is God.

In this passage, the title of "son of perdition" is used to identify the Antichrist. This is the only other time the term is used. Is Judas the Antichrist? Will we see him resurrected and ruling the world? Is hell "his own place?" Is hell his kingdom? Or, is he a saint who sacrificed his name and reputation in order to help Jesus save the human race?

Thus goes the polarity of thought concerning Judas as viewed between the Gospel of Judas and the Biblical account.

Whatever Judas' nature may be, we know he was a man placed in a position to turn the entire human history with a single act. He was a spiritual force. He was the executioner with his hand firmly on the trigger of prophecy.

Right and wrong hinge on intent. The same action may occur with opposite reasons in mind. It is the intent behind the action that determines right from wrong. One may kill to protect or to destroy. Both acts result in death but one is forgivable and at time even laudable. The other results in punishment and retribution. It is not the actions of Judas that we debate. Both sources, Bible and Gospel, reflect the same action. It is his intent that we attempt to discern.

Yet, it is possible to miss the larger picture. Jesus, the vessel of the Christ-spirit, selected a man to carry out his prophecy and his wishes.

Judas' Reward

Mat. 19:28

27 Then answered Peter and said unto him, Behold, we have forsaken all, and followed thee; what shall we have therefore?

28 And Jesus said unto them, Verily I say unto you, That ye which have followed me, in the regeneration when the Son of man shall sit in the throne of his glory, ye also shall sit upon twelve thrones, judging the twelve tribes of Israel.

Gospel of Judas 26. Jesus answered and said to him, "Come, that I (may show you the kingdom you will receive. I will show you the what is to come of you and this generation, but that you will be grieved when you see the kingdom and all its generation."

When Judas heard Him he said to him, "What good is it that I have received it? You have set me apart for that generation."

Jesus answered and said, "You will become the

128

thirteenth, and you will be cursed by the other generations, and you will come to rule over them. In the last days they will curse your ascent to the holy (generation / kingdom)."

It seems most odd that a Biblical account of Judas would have Jesus proclaiming to the twelve disciples that their reward would be exultation and the position of judges over the tribes of Israel. Judas was present in this conversation and Jesus addresses them as a group. The statement seems to be a direct contradiction at first, but Jesus throws in a condition and makes room for exclusions.

Let's look at the condition. "...**ye which have followed me, in the regeneration when the Son of man shall sit in the throne of his glory...**"

Even though Jesus addresses all twelve as a group, he does not say that they will all be rulers. He tells them that if they follow him their reward will be given when he comes to power and sits on the throne of his glory. The fact that this condition was given leads one to believe there was a reason it should exist and therefore all twelve sitting there may not follow him. However, Jesus does tell them there will be twelve men sitting on twelve thrones, judging the twelve tribes. If Judas is not counted in this number it would only leave Mathias or Paul to take his place. The Greek has the word translated as "ye" as a plural, leaving the simplest explanation counting Judas in the number of those judging the tribes but this is not so considering that 1Cor:15:5 states that Jesus appeared to Cephas, and then to the twelve. This was after Judas was dead and Mathias had taken his place.

In contrast, the Gospel of Judas is very direct and clear. Jesus tells Judas, **"You will become the thirteenth, and you will be cursed by the other generations, and you will come to rule over them. In the last days they will curse your ascent to the holy (generation / kingdom)."**

Judas will come to rule over them, but who is "them?" Is it the other disciples or could it be the "other generations?" This makes a huge difference. If we take the statement literally, we have to read it has Judas taking rulership over the other generations. These are the generations that did not receive the divine knowledge or that were assigned souls from Michael. If this is the case it does not necessarily contradict the Biblical account since the Antichrist will indeed rule over those whom did not receive the saving knowledge of Jesus.

But what about his accent to the "holy" generation?

In the Gnostic cosmology Jesus was sent by the

Great One and not by the creator of the material world. Antichrist is a term used in Greek that is not used in the same way as orthodox teaching as indoctrinated us to use. The word indicates some one or some thing that is a replacement for or is in opposition to the anointed one, but whose anointed one becomes the question. The problem with Gnosticism is a reversal of roles. In Gnostic theology Jesus did not come from the makers of this world but from one above the maker. Therefore, the one anointed by the maker is himself evil. If Jesus were sent by the Demiurge, Jesus would be evil. If one were against the anointed one of the Demiurge this person or Antichrist would be good in the Gnostic view. So, the Antichrist of the church was the savior of the Gnostics.

This idea is driven home when the place and purpose of Satan, the ultimate Antichrist, is examined through Gnostic eyes.

Satan's temptation to eat of the forbidden fruit is seen, not as temptation but as a way of salvation presented to Eve. This is because it offered Adam and Even "Knowledge" or Gnosis, which is salvation to Gnostics. Irenaeus tells us of others who regarded the tree of knowledge of good and evil as "Gnosis itself." This is a good example of why historians such as Roland H. Bainton have concluded that although Gnosticism absorbed much of the tradition of the Hebrews, it nevertheless "completely reversed their values."

Even if Judas was the "son of perdition" and Satan himself, he would be a liberator under the Gnostic tenants.

John 17

11 And now I am no more in the world, but these are in the world, and I come to thee. Holy Father, keep through thine own name those whom thou hast given me, that they may be one, as we are.

12 While I was with them in the world, I kept them in thy name: those that thou gavest me I have kept, and none of them is lost, but the son of perdition; that the scripture might be fulfilled.

2 Thessalonians 2

1 Now we beseech you, brethren, by the coming of our Lord Jesus Christ, and by our gathering together unto him,

2 That ye be not soon shaken in mind, or be troubled, neither by spirit, nor by word, nor by letter as from us, as that the day of Christ is at hand.

3 Let no man deceive you by any means: for that day

shall not come, except there come a falling away first, and that man of sin be revealed, the son of perdition;

4 Who opposeth and exalteth himself above all that is called God, or that is worshipped; so that he as God sitteth in the temple of God, shewing himself that he is God.

5 Remember ye not, that, when I was yet with you, I told you these things?

6 And now ye know what withholdeth that he might be revealed in his time.

7 For the mystery of iniquity doth already work: only he who now letteth will let, until he be taken out of the way.

8 And then shall that Wicked be revealed, whom the Lord shall consume with the spirit of his mouth, and shall destroy with the brightness of his coming:

9 Even him, whose coming is after the working of Satan with all power and signs and lying wonders,

10 And with all deceivableness of unrighteousness in them that perish; because they received not the love of the truth, that they might be saved.

Was Judas the incarnation of Satan? Is it the face of Judas we will be looking into when finally the Anti-Christ is revealed? The scriptures seem to imply just that.

The Setup

Was Jesus God? Was he the son of God? Was he omnipotent? Did he understand what was going to befall him? Did he know what Judas was planning?

To answer yes to any of these questions would shift the betrayal and death of Jesus away from the act of a single scoundrel into mutual culpability. If a person knows that an action will occur resulting in death and does nothing to prevent it, even our civil laws view this as negligent homicide... or in the case of Jesus, suicide.

John 6:70 Jesus answered them, Have not I chosen you twelve, and one of you is a devil?
71 He spake of Judas Iscariot the son of Simon: for he it was that should betray him, being one of the twelve.
John 13: 27: Then after the morsel, Satan entered into him. Jesus said to him, "What you are going to do, do quickly."

If one believes in Jesus' divinity, his power, of even his common sense, it must be assumed that he knew what was about to happen. He foretold the occurrence. He forewarned his disciples. He dismissed Judas from the

Passover meal and commanded him to " do what he was going to do and do it quickly."

The only question remaining is that one invoked by the Gospel of Judas. Was the unfolding scene leading to the crucifixion being allow to happen or was it being actively orchestrated?

Both the Gospel of Judas and the canonical gospels state that Jesus was fully aware of the future events. We are left to wonder if Jesus came to Judas and asked him to do this deed of betrayal so that scripture could be fulfilled or if Jesus simple chose Judas knowing his nature would lead to this end.

Judas' actions were small and probably insignificant in the overall scheme of things. The Jewish leaders were already planning the demise of Jesus. They would have already captured him if it weren't for their fear of causing a civil disturbance. They decided to wait until Jesus was out of sight and away from the town's people. Jesus points this out to the arresting guards in Luke 22:53.

So, we are left knowing that Judas brought the authorities to a place where Jesus frequented to capture a man they had already decided to arrest and whom they saw every day in town or at the temple. We are told that Jesus knew what was about to happen. We are also told that Jesus told Judas when to act.

Excluding the divergent theologies of the Gospel of Judas and the canonical gospels, there remains only one simple question; that of "why." What motivated Judas? Why did he do this unthinkable thing?

Jesus told him to do it. This is true in both stories. Jesus was aware of the plan. He had the ability to stop the scenario at any time.

Did Jesus use Judas to fulfill prophecy, knowing his greedy nature, or did he use Judas, knowing his devotion? Either way, Judas took the fall.

Bibliography and Resources

The Maecenas Foundation for Ancient Art, April 2006
The Gospel of Judas
Coptic text established by
Rodolphe Kasser and Gregor Wurst

The Gospel of Judas (Hardcover)
by National Geographic Society (Author), Bart D. Ehrman
(Commentary), Rodolphe Kasser (Editor), Marvin Meyer
(Editor), Gregor Wurst (Editor)
ISBN-13: 978-1426200427

Reading Judas: The Gospel of Judas and the Shaping of
Christianity (Hardcover)
by Elaine Pagels (Author), Karen L. King (Author)
Publisher: Viking Adult (March 6, 2007)
ISBN-13: 978-0670038459

The Gospel of Judas, Critical Edition: Together with the
Letter of Peter to Phillip, James, and a Book of Allogenes
from Codex Tchacos (Hardcover)
by Rodolphe Kasser (Author), Gregor Wurst (Author)
ISBN-13: 978-1426201912

Joseph B. Lumpkin

Judas and the Gospel of Jesus: Have We Missed the Truth
about Christianity? (Hardcover)
by N. T. Wright (Author)
Publisher: Baker Books (October 1, 2006)
 ISBN-10: 0801012945

Various Coptic language resources.

All Bible quotes are from the King James Version.

ABOUT THE AUTHOR

Joseph Lumpkin has written over a dozen books on subjects such as religion, theology, and counseling. He has written for various newspapers and is the author of the best selling book, *The Lost Book Of Enoch: A Comprehensive Transliteration*, published by Fifth Estate Publishers.

Joseph holds his Doctorate in the field of Ministry. He lives near Birmingham, Alabama with his wife, Lynn, and his son, Breandan.

Look for other fine books by Joseph Lumpkin.

The Lost Book Of Enoch: A Comprehensive Transliteration,
ISBN: 0974633666

The Book of Jubilees; The Little Genesis, The Apocalypse of
Moses
ISBN: 193358009

The Book Of Jasher
The J. H. Parry Text in Modern English
ISBN: 1933580143

The Gnostic Gospels of Philip, Mary Magdalene, and Thomas
ISBN: 1933580135

The Gospel of Thomas: A Contemporary Translation
ISBN: 0976823349

Fallen Angels, The Watchers, and the Origins of Evil:
A Problem of Choice
ISBN: 1933580100

Joseph B. Lumpkin

End of Days: The Apocalyptic Writings
The Apocalypse of Abraham, The Apocalypse of Thomas, or
The Revelation of Thomas, 4 Ezra, also referred to as 2
Esdras or the Apocalypse of Ezra, 2 Baruch, also known as
the Syriac. Apocalypse of Baruch
ISBN: 1-933580-38-0

Dark Night of the Soul - A Journey to the Heart of God
ISBN: 0974633631

The Tao Te Ching: A Contemporary Translation
ISBN: 0976823314

Christian Counseling – Healing the Tribes of Man
ISBN: 1933589970

www.ingramcontent.com/pod-product-compliance
Lightning Source LLC
Chambersburg PA
CBHW072152090426
42740CB00012B/2242